SOUTH ASIAN CULTURE
&
Islam

Uzma Hussain

Bismillahir Rahmanir Raheem

Greenbird Books

London

First published in Great Britain in 2012 by Greenbird Books
Text © 2012 by Uzma Hussain
Cover Art © 2012 by Greenbird Books
Graphics © 2012 EclectiCollections
This book has been typeset in Georgia
Printed in USA
British Library Cataloguing in Publication Data:
A catalogue record for this book is available from the
British Library.

ISBN: 978-0-9571995-5-2

www.greenbirdbooks.com

Contents

Acknowledgments

In the name of Allah, Most Gracious, Most Merciful.
Praise is only for Allah,
Lord of the Universe;
Most Kind, Most Merciful;
Master of the Day of Judgment.
You alone we worship,
And to you alone we pray for help.
Show us the straight way,
The way of those whom you have blessed,
Who have not deserved your anger,
Nor gone astray.
[Quran, Al-Fatiha (The Opening), 1:1–7]

I express my humble gratitude to Allah Almighty who provided me with the resources to write this book. I am enormously grateful to each and every individual who has contributed in the overall project, from research to translation, strict editing to proofreading and photography to book design. I'd like to express my most sincere thanks for all your tremendous support, encouragement and valuable suggestions. May Allah Almighty reward you all in abundance. All good and perfection is for Allah Almighty and any mistakes herein are mine. I welcome comments and feedback by the readers for future reviews or editing.

Introduction

The believers, men and women
Are protectors of one another: they enjoin
What is just, and forbid
What is evil: they observe
Regular prayers, practise
Regular charity, and obey
Allah and His Messenger.
On them will Allah pour
His mercy: for Allah
Is Exalted, Wise.
[Quran, Al-Tawba (Repentance), 9:71]

All praise and thanks be to Allah Almighty, Lord of the worlds, the Beneficent, the Merciful. Peace and blessings be upon our beloved Prophet Muhammad, and all those who follow his example.

In this book, we have sought to address some vital issues especially relevant to the many South Asian Muslim communities living in the Indian subcontinent and in other parts of the world. Our research involved discussions with South Asians in Pakistan, the United Kingdom and the United States over a period of nine years. Through our work we have noticed a disturbing pattern of very traditional and cultural practices driving young South Asian women to rebel and turn against their *deen* (religion). The young women are oppressed in the name of Islam by those who have strong loyalty to Indian cultural traditions which have been carried down from generation to generation. The oppression felt by many young South Asian Muslims in fact goes against the Islamic teachings of the Quran and the *sunnah*.

This book has been produced to serve as a religious and moral guideline. It aims to provide clear information and evidence from the authentic, original sources of the Quran and the *sunnah*, and to address the underlying root causes of many of the cultural and social issues that confront South Asian Muslims.

Our objective is to bring about an awareness of Islamic rights with a special emphasis on the rights of Muslim women, so that much of the oppression they face may be eradicated, and they may feel confident and strong in their Muslim identity. Although the domestic, social and cultural ramifications outlined may be sensitive, they are the very reasons why a large proportion of South Asian Muslim families are failing to make good economic, social, moral and educational progress.

In order for there to be justice, reform and progress, it is necessary to first distinguish between oppressive culture and the true beauty of the real *deen*. It is indeed the true essence of Islam that liberated women from oppression over 1400 years ago. Today women are being denied their natural Islamic rights by those who have distorted Islam to cater for their loyalty to Indian cultural practices. In order to find the truth, one has to turn to the original source of the Quran and the *sunnah*. This book is written to help South Asian Muslims understand their rights and reclaim that which Allah Almighty has bestowed upon believing men and women.

The topics in the book give a special emphasis to the Islamic rights of newlywed women. It is these women who are the cradle of civilisation: they are the first teachers of their children. If these women are oppressed, the community will remain ignorant and oppressed.

It is an obligation to purify Islam from misunderstandings and misinterpretations. Any practice that leads to injustice and oppression cannot be accepted upon religious, social or moral principles within the *shariah*.

The Messenger of Allah (peace be upon him) said this about purifying the *sunnah*:

> This knowledge will be carried by the trustworthy ones of every generation – they will expel from it the alteration made by those going beyond bounds, the false claims of the liars, and the false interpretations of the ignorant.
> [Ibn 'Adiyy, al-Khatib al Baghdadi, Ibn Asakir, and others]

1

Marriage

Marriage opens the doors to fulfil some of the most basic human needs of companionship, happiness, respect, compassion, and friendship, as well as fulfilling sexual desire. It also brings responsibility and commitment. Correct knowledge and preparation is the key to a successful marriage where there is love, understanding, respect and harmony between the spouses. This success begins with the intention: in order for the spouses to secure a loving relationship, they must intend to attain the greatest love of all – to marry for the pleasure of Allah Almighty.

It is related on the authority of Umar ibn al-Khattab (may Allah be pleased with him) who said:

> I heard the Messenger of Allah (peace be upon him) say:
> 'Actions are only (judged) by intention and every man will
> have that which he intended.'
> [Al-Bukhari, Muslim]

The Prophet (peace be upon him) spoke about marriage as 'half the religion'. Marriage is an institution which brings a man and a woman together to enjoy each other's company, support one another through mutual understanding, and co-operate as a team. The foundation of a successful marriage starts by choosing the right partner: the one whom you can grow to love and respect, and with whom you can strive to bring up the next generation in a caring environment, influencing them with compassion, values, and your own example. Creating stable family units in a harmonious environment in turn creates a prosperous society.

A marriage is a solemn agreement between the man and the woman. It must only be contracted in writing when both the man and the woman have given their full and free consent to marry each other.

Islam gives both men and women the right to accept or refuse a marriage proposal. Islam prohibits forced marriages, deeming them unlawful and invalid. Forced marriages that take place in some South Asian homes in the name of Islam only make the young men and women rebellious towards their religion. Youngsters are made to believe that their parents are carrying out their Islamic duty by forcibly marrying them. Each individual should seek to understand the rights and responsibilities in a marriage as ignorance can lead a person astray and deprive the person of the rewards of the Hereafter.

Allah Almighty says:

> O you who believe!
> You are forbidden to inherit women against their will.
> [Quran, Al-Nisa (Women), 4:19]

One of the chapters from *Sahih Bukhari* is significantly titled: 'When a man gives his daughter in marriage and she dislikes it, the marriage shall be annulled.'

There are many examples of the Messenger of Allah (peace be upon him) honouring this right when women approached him about a forced marriage. One example is of a woman called Khansa bint Khidam who complained to the Messenger of Allah (peace be upon him) about her marriage:

> My father married me to his nephew, and I did not like this match, so I complained to the Messenger of Allah (peace be upon him). He (peace be upon him) said to me: 'Accept what your father has arranged.' I said, 'I do not wish to accept what my father has arranged.' He (peace be upon him) said, this marriage is invalid, go and marry whomever

you wish.' I said, 'I have accepted what my father has arranged, but I wanted women to know that fathers have no power in the matter.'
[Al-Bukhari]

No-one can force a man or a woman into a marriage against their will as each individual is responsible and accountable for his or her own life, deeds and actions.

The Messenger of Allah (peace be upon him) said:

A woman without a husband must not be married until she is consulted, and a virgin must not be married till her permission is asked.
[Al-Bukhari, Muslim]

When a man or a woman is ready to marry, they should choose a partner who will help and support them on the right path. Choosing the wrong partner can have serious consequences in this world and in the Hereafter.

The Prophet (peace be upon him) said:

A woman is married for four reasons: her wealth, her family status, her beauty and her religion. So you should marry the religious woman (otherwise) you will be a loser.
[Al-Bukhari]

When choosing a spouse, people look at materialism, family honour and customs, but the Messenger of Allah (peace be upon him) emphasised the high importance of choosing a pious spouse for blessings in this world and success in the Hereafter.

One may also wish to consider the family background, friends and the living environment of a prospective spouse, as characteristics, habits and personality are important when looking into the compatibility of a marital relationship. For the woman, an ideal husband would be one who is pious,God-fearing and of good character.

One should not be misled by the appearance of a person just because the man looks religious and prays, but also be satisfied that he is of good character. The Prophet (peace be upon him) emphasised the importance of good character in the following *hadiths:*

The believers with the most complete *imaan* [faith] are those with the best character.
[Abu Dawud]

If someone whose piety and character you are satisfied with approaches you for marriage, accept his request. If you do not, there will be trials in the earth and a great deal of evil.
[Al-Tirmidhi]

2

Financial responsibility

It is all too common practice in some South Asian communities for boys to marry young and then leave their newlyweds with their families while they go away to work. Sometimes a man marries and leaves his wife in his brother's or parent's home because he does not have the financial means or resources to support his own wife. Being left alone to live with the husband's family, the new bride can sometimes find herself in situations which result in friction and aggravation between her and the family. These women have to face such dilemmas alone and risk falling into depression.

Allah Almighty says:

And let those who find not
The financial means for marriage
Keep themselves chaste, until
Allah enriches them of his bounty.
[Quran, Al-Nur (Light), 24:33]

The husband himself must strive and work to support his own wife and his children. If he does not yet have the financial means to support a wife, then he should not enter the marriage contract, but remain patient and chaste.

Al-Bukhari relates the following conversation between a man and the Messenger of Allah (peace be upon him):

'By Allah, it is better for one of you to go in the morning, collect firewood, carry it on his back, and sell it to suffice himself and give charity from it, than it is to go to a man

5

beg – whether he gives or denies him. That is because the upper (giving) hand is better than the lower (taking) hand. And start giving to those for whom you are responsible.'A man asked, 'For whom am I responsible, O Allah's Messenger?'

The Messenger of Allah (peace be upon him) replied, 'Your wife is of those for whom you are responsible, as well as your slave girl and your child.'

[Al-Bukhari, Muslim]

The man must enter a marriage in full knowledge of his financial responsibility towards his wife. When a man signs the marriage contract, he commissions himself to take on the responsibility of his wife and becomes her guardian.

Allah Almighty says:

Men are protectors and maintainers of women,
Because God has given the one more (strength)
Than the other, and because
They support them from their means.
Therefore righteous women are devoutly obedient, and guard
In (the husband's absence) what Allah would have them guard
(honour, property, secrets, etc.).
[Quran, Al-Nisa (Women), 4:34]

Allah Almighty establishes and commands husbands to protect, maintain and support their wives before ordering the women to obey their husbands (within the Islamic context) and safeguard the husband's home. The wife is also responsible for looking after the children, steering them onto the right path, and attending to the affairs of the home. A husband's responsibility includes providing his children with good, beneficial education. Both the man and the woman play an equally important role to create a strong, healthy family unit which contributes to society.

Allah Almighty says:

> Let the women live
> In the same style as you live
> According to your means,
> Annoy them not, so as
> To restrict them.
> [Quran, Al-Talaq (Divorce), 65:6]

In order to create a successful, happy marriage, the husband who has commissioned himself to protect and take care of his wife through *nikah* (marriage), has taken on the responsibility of ensuring that his wife enjoys an equal status to himself. He must provide her with a safe and secure dwelling where she must not be subjected to harassment, abuse, torture, ill treatment or any harm by anyone, whether it is mental, psychological or physical. The above verse of the Quran applies to a wife in general as well as during an *iddah* period (waiting period) of a woman.

Allah Almighty says:

> Nor should you treat them (wives) with harshness...
> [Quran, Al-Nisa (Women), 4:19]

If the husband is a rich man, he must spend generously upon his wife and if he is a poor man, he must spend accordingly. Amongst other things the husband must provide for his wife and children the following: lodgings, food, clothing, medicine, and education. Allah Almighty says:

> Let the man of means
> Spend according to
> His means: and the man
> Whose resources are restricted,
> Let him spend according
> To what Allah has given him.
> [Quran, Al-Talaq (Divorce), 65:7]

3

The wife can maintain her own identity

A wife has the right to keep her father's name after marriage and not to have to take on her husband's name, so that her lineage is recognised.

For example, when the Messenger of Allah (peace be upon him) married Aisha (may Allah be pleased with her), who was the daughter of Abu Bakr Siddiq (may Allah be pleased with him), the identity of Aisha did not change and her name remained Aisha Siddiq or Aisha bint Abu Bakr Siddiq. The lineage of Aisha, who was the wife of the Messenger of Allah (peace be upon him), is recognised by her father's name.

When Fatima (may Allah be pleased with her), who was the daughter of the Messenger of Allah (peace be upon him), married Ali bin Abi Talib (may Allah be pleased with him), she was still called Fatima bint Muhammad. After marriage, Fatima's surname did not change to her husband's name. The wife's lineage is therefore recognised through her father's name.

The change of names can cause many problems when identifying the person. The chopping and changing of names on official documents has also led to confusion, especially when a woman has married more than once. Women who go through multiple marriages find it very difficult to explain their correct identity because with each marriage they take on their husband's name, leading to complications over their own identity.

Asmaa bint Umaais was one of the female companions of the

Messenger of Allah (peace be upon him). Asmaa bint Umaais married Jafar Tayyar bin Abi Talib. Jafar was the brother of Ali bin Abi Talib. After Jafar Tayyar bin Abi Talib was martyred, the Messenger of Allah (peace be upon him) solemnised her *nikah* with Abu Bakr Siddiq (may Allah be pleased with him). After Abu Bakr Siddiq passed away in the year 13AH, Asmaa bint Umaais married Ali bin Abi Talib (may Allah be pleased with him).

Asmaa bint Umaais did not change her name to any of her husbands' names. Thus, a woman has the right to retain her own name throughout her life.

4

Mahr [dowry]

The Arabic word for dowry is *mahr*. In the *shariah* (Islamic law), *mahr* is given by the husband to the wife. The word dowry used in this chapter refers to *mahr* and is not to be confused with the meaning referred to in the Indian subcontinent, where lavish gifts are given from the bride to the bridegroom, as such a practice goes totally against Islamic principles.

Mahr is given to the woman by her husband as a gesture of love and a realisation of his financial responsibility towards her. When a man signs the marriage contract, he commissions himself with the responsibility to provide complete maintenance, *mahr*, support, protection, food, clothing, dwelling etc. for his wife.
Allah Almighty says:

> Give women their dowries as an outright gift.
> [Quran, Al-Nisa (Women), 4:4]

Many South Asian families have a corrupt practice that destroys the true essence of a harmonious marriage – that is to expect and demand gifts from the bride's family. Many brides are treated harshly if they do not bring sufficient gifts into the in-laws' household.

The Messenger of Allah (peace be upon him) did not give anything at his daughter Fatima's wedding to his son-in-law Ali (may Allah be pleased with them), nor to his mother, nor to any other member of Ali's family. The Messenger of Allah (peace be upon him) only prayed for Ali; no gifts were distributed to Ali or his family.

The Messenger of Allah (peace be upon him) gave his daughter only a few gifts for her to use in her home where she and her husband were to live.

Any gifts that are given to the bride from her parents are exclusively hers and no-one has the right to take them away from her; if she wishes to share her gifts, she may, but should only do so of her own free will.

If parents do provide gifts for their daughter, this should not be made into a display to show off or to compete, and it is not for anyone to enquire about what has been given. It is not for anyone to be offended because they have not been told or consulted on what should be given. The gifts given to the daughter by her parents are simply no-one else's concern.

The *mahr* to the Prophet's daughter, Fatima, from her husband, Ali, was 400 dirhams. Allah Almighty has not laid down any limit to how much or how little *mahr* a woman can stipulate for her marriage to be contracted. Allah Almighty says:

> And if you wish to replace a wife with another
> And even you have given one of them a heap of gold,
> Take not the least bit back,
> Would you take it as a fraud and a clear sin?
> [Quran, Al-Nisa (Women), 4:20]

Let us look at this following story of Mustafa and Sadia as an example:

A young man by the name of Mustafa wants to marry a lady called Sadia. Mustafa proposes to Sadia and approaches Sadia's father as her wali, or guardian, for his approval to marry his daughter. Sadia's father therefore asks his daughter's permission regarding this proposal for her marriage. Sadia gives her consent to marrying Mustafa. Sadia's parents and Mustafa's parents are happy for the marriage of Mustafa and Sadia to take place.

Sadia wishes to stipulate on the marriage contract that she wants mahr of £3,000 to be given immediately; she does not want the mahr to be deferred. Mustafa agrees to pay the mahr of £3,000 to take Sadia as his bride.

It is highly recommended by the Messenger of Allah (peace be upon him) that the amount of mahr should be clearly stated on the marriage contract, as this prevents disagreements over the amount that was agreed.

In this case, if Mustafa had said that the agreed mahr was £2,000, and Sadia had said that the agreed mahr was £4,000, the written contract stipulating the amount of mahr (signed by both Mustafa and Sadia at their nikah) would have clarified the amount of mahr that they actually agreed.

Mustafa and Sadia want to have their nikah (marriage ceremony) and walima the next month. Mustafa and Sadia do not wish to waste money on unnecessary materialistic gifts and imitations of other cultural ceremonies, because they know that they will be accountable for their actions in front of Allah Almighty. Therefore, there is no prior engagement or henna ceremony etc. that would involve unnecessary expenditure. Instead Mustafa spends his money on buying and moderately furnishing their new home. Mustafa and Sadia are aware of their obligations towards one another.

When Sadia and Mustafa's marriage takes place, Sadia receives £3,000 of the agreed mahr from her husband, Mustafa. This £3,000 exclusively belongs to Sadia and no-one has any right to take away any of it from Sadia, including her husband, unless Sadia of her own free will should wish to give any of it.

Many South Asian women lose out on their God-given right to receive *mahr* altogether. They should stipulate on the marriage contract how much *mahr* they want from their husbands. Sometimes they lose out because the *mahr* is deferred against their will by members of their own families. Many wives are never paid at all.

In some rare cases, a bride's own parents stipulate a large amount of *mahr* on their daughter's marriage contract, knowing that her future husband cannot afford it. They state that the *mahr* will only be paid if the husband should divorce their daughter. The parents do this to ensure that their daughter is never divorced.

Here are some examples of how such a practice works against the principles of Islam:

- The father is denying his daughter her right to receive *mahr* from her husband.
- A wife is under the care, protection, and support of her husband. It is forbidden for a man to keep a wife with the intent to cause her any harm, injury or ill treatment; otherwise he will be acting against Allah's commands. Therefore it is better for a husband to divorce his wife than to commit any wrong by keeping her.
- It is better for her own welfare for her to be divorced than to live an oppressed life with him.

Allah Almighty says:

> You are forbidden to inherit
> Women against their will.
> Nor should you treat them with harshness...
> [Quran, Al-Nisa (Women), 4:19]

Allah Almighty has commanded that men either keep their wives in kindness or release them in kindness:

> The parties should either hold with correctness and courtesy
> Or separate with kindness.
> [Quran, Al-Baqara (Cow), 2:229]

Many South Asian husbands try to escape giving *mahr* or providing maintenance for their wives, but ironically they and their families expect gifts from the bride's family. As a result of this, many Asian fathers go into lifelong debt by borrowing loans in order to have their daughters married. Many other fathers have gone as far as to accept bribery.

This culture from the Indian subcontinent is oppressive and damages the true Islamic marriage. It not only affects the women but also the men, since they are the ones who become fathers, earning for their own daughters' dowries – sometimes in unlawful ways. If they are unable to meet the expectations of the in-laws of providing lavish ceremonies and generous gifts, their daughters suffer harsh treatment and taunts from their in-laws. Consequently, this South Asian culture contributes to a corrupt, weak and failing society.

5

Seeking permission to enter

When a Muslim wishes to enter anyone's home other than his own, there is a certain Islamic etiquette that must be followed. No-one should enter someone else's home without first seeking permission from the dwellers of the house. The way to do this is to stand at the side of the door and not directly in front of it, so that the visitor cannot look inside, as they may see something unlawful, such as a person within the home who may not be dressed appropriately.

The companion of the Messenger of Allah (peace be upon him), Abdullah ibn Busr, said:

> Whenever the Prophet (peace be upon him) came to a door
> seeking permission to enter, he did not stand facing it; he
> would stand to the right or the left. If he was given permission,
> he would enter, otherwise he would leave.
> [Al-Bukhari]

Allah Almighty says:

> O you who believe!
> Enter not houses other than
> Your own, until you have
> Asked permission and saluted
> Those in them,
> That is best for you, in order that
> You may heed.

If you find no-one
In the house, enter not
Until permission is given
To you: if you are asked
To go back, go back:
That makes for greater purity
For yourselves: and Allah
Knows well all that you do.

[Quran, Al-Nur (Light), 24:27–28]

A Muslim visitor, male or female, is commanded to say salaam and then seek permission to enter. Only if they are given permission, should they enter. If permission to enter is refused or there is no answer, the visitor must go back and should not feel angry or upset even if the dwellers are at home.

Allah Almighty tells Muslims to also teach their children who have reached the age of puberty to seek permission before entering anyone else's home.

The Messenger of Allah (peace be upon him) would not even enter his own children's houses without seeking permission first. If the Messenger of Allah (peace be upon him) was told to go back, he would go back.

Here is another example of how a visitor such as Abu Bakr (may Allah be pleased with him) would enter a house other than his own. He entered by permission from the dwellers of the house, who happened to be Fatima (may Allah be pleased with her), the daughter of the Messenger of Allah, and her husband, Ali (may Allah be pleased with him).

Abu Bakr went to Fatima when she was ill and asked permission to enter. Ali said (to Fatima):

'Abu Bakr is at the door. Do you wish to give permission?'
She said, 'Do you agree to that?' He said, 'Yes.'

[Muhammad Ibn Sa'd, *The Women of Madina*, p. 19. Publisher: Ta-Ha.]

There are some visitors who start to look at the side of the house, or behind the house, or even through the window if there is no response at the door. They may start looking through keyholes, or over fences, and even go as far as to climb over the walls. This behaviour goes against the commands of Allah Almighty and against the teachings of the *sunnah*.

The Messenger of Allah (peace be upon him) said in public:

> If a person peeps into somebody else's house without
> permission, the people of the house will be justified to injure
> his eye.
> [Muslim]

Islam teaches Muslims to respect other people's privacy. The dwellers of a house may not be in a state to receive visitors. If the house happens to be empty, a visitor cannot enter without seeking permission from its owner, no matter where the owner is.

It is not permitted to try to look inside someone else's home. If there is no answer at the door, the visitor should not try to find a way in, or peep inside to see if someone is at home. Instead, the visitor should leave quietly without feeling offended or annoyed, even if the resident is at home but does not wish to let the visitor in.

The laws of Islam for seeking permission before entering someone's house are to give the residents privacy and tranquillity within their own homes.

Allah Almighty says:

> But when the children among you
> Come of age, let them (also)
> Ask for permission, as do those
> Senior to them (in age).
> [Quran, Al-Nur (Light), 24:59]

Parents must teach their children who have reached the age of puberty to seek permission before entering someone else's home.

When children have reached puberty, it is also not permissible for their parents to see any part of their child's body that is not lawful for them to see. The parents must also seek permission before entering upon their child who has reached the age of puberty.

It is only under certain exceptional circumstances that it is otherwise, such as when it may be a necessity to look at a part of the body for medical reasons.

> The Messenger of Allah (peace be upon him) told the men not
> to call upon women when they are alone. When a companion
> asked, 'O Messenger of Allah, what about the younger or
> elder brother of the husband?'
> The Messenger of Allah (peace be upon him) said, 'He is death.'
> [Al-Tirmidhi, Al-Bukhari, Muslim]

This shows the prohibition against a non-*mahrem* man – a man who is not closely related and with whom marriage is permissible – from entering the houses of women. There is an especially strong prohibition placed upon a brother-in-law from entering the home of his brother's wife when she is alone to avoid any temptation or accusations of infidelity.

The South Asian joint family culture is not in compliance with Islamic law. Often, various members of one family walk freely through the rooms and bedrooms of another member living in the same house. This way of living does not comply with the commands of Allah Almighty and is not in line with the teachings of the *sunnah*. Consideration must be given to another person's privacy, security and tranquillity, in accordance with the *shariah*.

6

The wife's mother

In many South Asian families, there is a misconception that the mother-in-law replaces the wife's own mother, or that the wife should give the mother-in-law a higher status than her own mother. The wife's mother is deprived of receiving love and attention from her own daughter as though she does not exist.

The daughter-in-law's own mother, who carried her in her womb for nine months, gave birth to her, weaned her and raised her, will always have rights over her, and her own daughter will have rights over her own mother.

There are no obligatory religious duties towards a mother-in-law from a daughter-in-law or a son-in-law, but they should treat their mother-in-law as an elder with respect and consideration. As an elder, the mother-in-law too should treat her daughter-in-law and son-in-law with compassion and consideration.

The Messenger of Allah (peace be upon him) said:

> He does not belong to us [Muslims] who is not kind to our
> young and does not respect our old.
> [Al-Tirmidhi]

A wife can visit her parents with her husband's consent but she does not need permission from the husband's parents to go outdoors, as some South Asian in-laws demand. The daughter should not be deprived of visiting her own parents, showing them kindness and offering her services to them.

When the mother of Asma, daughter of Abu Bakr, was still a

disbeliever and she came to visit her daughter, Asma asked the
Messenger of Allah (peace be upon him):

'O Messenger of Allah, my mother has come to see me.
Should I receive her and treat her with all the affection
that is her due?' The Messenger of Allah (peace be upon
him), replied, 'Yes, treat her with full affection.'
[Al-Bukhari, Muslim]

The wife's own mother should receive love and affection from
her own daughter just as the Messenger of Allah (peace be upon him)
commanded it in the case of Asma, the daughter of Abu Bakr. She
should offer her mother full affection even if her mother happens not
to be a Muslim.

It is fairly common amongst some South Asian families that
mothers are totally deprived of affection from their daughters after
they marry, and the daughters are deprived of their mothers' love.
A woman's mother does not become replaced by the husband's
mother.

Allah Almighty says:

In travail upon travail
Did his mother bear him
And his weaning is in two years:
Show gratitude
To Me and to your parents:
To Me is (your final) Goal.
[Quran, Luqman (Luqman), 31:14]

A mother will always have rights over her own children and vice
versa. The children have obligations towards their parents who raised
them. If a husband or a wife does any good for their spouse's parents,
it is great *sadaqa* (charitable deed) for both of them and carries great
reward, but it is not a religious duty.

It is well known amongst South Asian Muslims that a husband's father becomes a *mahrem* to his son's wife, but some men have not grasped that when they marry, they too became *mahrem* to their wife's mother. It is therefore permissible for the wife's mother to perform a pilgrimage such as Hajj accompanied by their daughter's husband as a *mahrem*.

If a wife does any good deed for her husband's parents that pleases the husband, it pleases Allah Almighty and carries great reward. Just the same, if the husband does any good deed for his wife's parents that pleases his wife, it pleases Allah Almighty and it too carries great reward.

7

Joint family culture is not supported by the Quran

BACKGROUND HISTORY

Pakistan, India and Bangladesh were all one nation. For generations, the Muslims, Sikhs, and Hindus lived together under foreign rule until 1947, when India and Pakistan became two separate independent states.

For centuries under foreign rule, there had been much ignorance due to lack of education; in many regions people received no education at all. This led to a great deal of illiteracy, lack of knowledge and distorted information, which, in many parts of the Indian subcontinent, still exists even today. After the advent of Islam in India, the Indian Muslims had accepted some Islamic principles such as established prayer *(salah)*, fasting *(sawm)*, and pilgrimage (Hajj), but when it came to marriage, family and social life, they maintained many of the same Indian cultural traditions and rituals.

The Indian Muslims engaged in Hindu practices that are contrary to the teachings of Islam, such as the bridegroom receiving a dowry from the wife's family, and the wife going to live with the husband's family. In Hindu custom, brothers-in-law are treated like their own brothers. In Islam, these men are not *mahrem* and must be treated as non-*mahrem* men.

This cultural practice of the wife being sent off to live with the husband's parents and family is not from the Quran, nor is it from the *sunnah* of the Messenger of Allah (peace be upon him).

22

Our research shows that joint family culture is a culture practised by Hindus, Sikhs and Muslims originating from India prior to the partition of Pakistan and India.

Joint family culture is not generally practised amongst the Muslim Arab nations, including Saudi Arabia, nor is it practised in the Muslim world of Far East Asia, such as Malaysia or Indonesia. It is not practised in the Muslim countries in Europe, such as Turkey and Bosnia. It is also not generally practised in the very poor African Muslim countries, such as Sudan and Somalia, except in severe economic conditions.

RIGHT TO A SEPARATE DWELLING

The Messenger of Allah (peace be upon him) had four daughters: Zainab, Ruqayya, Umm Kulthum and the youngest daughter, Fatima, who all survived and married. All his other children had died. The daughters of the Messenger of Allah (peace be upon him) lived with their husbands after marriage in a house or quarters (apartment) separate from their in-laws.

Allah Almighty says:

> Lodge them (wives) according to what you reside out of your means,
> Do not harass them in order to make life difficult for them.
> [Quran, Al-Talaq (Divorce), 65:6]

The husband is obliged to provide his wife with a separate dwelling. The wife must not be subjected to any harassment or abuse from any member of the husband's family. If he cannot afford a house, he must provide his wife with a portion of a house or apartment that is exclusively hers, with its own separate entrance so that she can live in privacy and tranquillity.

No-one from the husband's family or her own family has the right to enter upon her without her permission (see Chapter 5

'Seeking permission to enter'). The Prophet (peace be upon him) would not enter anyone's home, including the homes of his own children, without seeking permission.

A husband's parents have no legal right to demand their son's wife lives with them unless she herself wishes to live with them. A daughter-in-law is a woman with her own personality. She should be free to express herself, her views, opinions, emotions and feelings, as with any human being, and not live in silent fear of her in-laws.

SIGNIFICANCE OF TRANQUILLITY

Allah Almighty commands that the husband and wife live in tranquillity to achieve the ideal family environment.
Allah Almighty says:

> And among His signs is this:
> That He created
> For you mates from amongst
> Yourselves that you may
> Dwell in tranquillity with them,
> And He has put love
> And mercy between your (hearts).
> Verily in that are Signs
> For those who reflect.
> [Quran, Al-Rum (The Byzantines), 30:21]

Tranquillity is a quality of peace where one finds calmness, repose and relaxation without disturbance.

Tranquillity within the home is necessary for a husband and wife to build a good, healthy, loving family unit. The children are greatly influenced and affected by how the parents interact with each other. A harmonious environment will encourage them to feel secure and become kind, confident and sincere human beings.

From the time a baby is born, it forms a naturally close, special and loving bond with its mother, whom it trusts for its nourishment and upbringing. The security and fulfilment of the wife is crucial for raising good, healthy, happy and confident children. The environment of a happy mother and her feelings are passed onto her children through the special mother-and-child bond. In the same way, the feelings and environment of an oppressed and distraught mother also are passed onto her children, making the children weak and insecure. A happy, fulfilled wife brings comfort, joy, compassion and relaxation within the home. This creates a harmonious environment that contributes to the character building, attitude and personal development of the children.

FAIRNESS AND JUSTICE

If there should arise a dispute between the husband and wife, they should be left to resolve their disagreement with mutual understanding, without external involvement. However, if they have failed to resolve their dispute, the couple can call for arbiters.

Islam is based on fairness and justice. The Quran makes it very clear that one arbiter must be brought from the husband's side and one from the wife's side. The job of the male arbiters from each side of the family is to establish whether the couple can patch up their differences.

Allah Almighty says:

> If you fear a breach between a couple,
> Send an arbiter from his people,
> And an arbiter from her people,
> If the couple desire to put things right,
> Allah will bring reconciliation between them.
> [Quran, Al-Nisa (Women), 4:35]

In reality, within some South Asian households there are several members living with the couple from the husband's side of the family who frequently interfere, but there is absolutely no-one from the wife's side to give any fair representation.

The ideal goals of a loving, happy Muslim marital relationship cannot be achieved if the wife is controlled and dominated by another woman or anyone else in the house claiming rule and authority over her and the home. Some mothers-in-law become jealous of the intimacy between their son and their daughter-in-law. The mother-in-law's pride and jealousy has clearly destroyed many happy marriages.

If the husband's mother curses her, the husband, too, may be influenced by his mother and fail to fulfil his obligatory duties towards his wife. In some cases, especially in rural villages, South Asian daughters-in-law are tortured and even set on fire by their in-laws,
mainly because they come from poor families. Any act that leads to oppression and brutality cannot be tolerated and it is the responsibility of Muslims as a whole, to rid their society of such injustices.

Allah Almighty tells the believers to deal with justice in all matters even when dealing amongst close relations:

> O you who believe!
> Stand out firmly
> For justice, as witnesses
> To God, even as against
> Yourselves, or your parents,
> Or your kin, and whether
> It be (against) rich or poor;
> For God's claim takes precedence over both.
> [Quran, Al-Nisa (Women), 4:135]

When a man enters into a marriage contract, he commissions himself to become fully responsible for his wife's welfare.

Allah Almighty says:

> Men are protectors and maintainers of women,
> Because God has given the one more (strength)

Than the other, and because
They support them from their means.
Therefore righteous women are devoutly obedient to their
husbands.

[Quran, Al-Nisa (Women), 4:34]

By entering the marriage contract, the husband has taken upon himself a duty to maintain, defend and protect his wife from any harm, injury, ill treatment or abuse, and therefore she has an obligation to obey her husband (within the Islamic context).

In the Messenger of Allah's (peace be upon him) farewell speech *(khutbah)* at Mount Arafat, he (peace be upon him) emphasised the importance of men's responsibility in taking care of their wives.

In his last sermon, the Messenger of Allah (peace be upon him) said:

Your treatment of your wives should be righteous and kind, for they are in your custody and cannot safeguard their rights. The day you married them, you considered them as a trust of Allah, and you brought them home according to His injunctions.

The Messenger of Allah (peace be upon him) enjoins the men to uphold the rights of their wives in accordance with the commands of Allah Almighty. The men have brought their wives home as a trust *(amanah)* from Allah Almighty, and have made a solemn pledge (the *nikah*) to Allah Almighty to take care of their wives in accordance with the commands of their Lord.

Allah Almighty says:

Live with them (your wives) in kindness;
If you dislike them, perhaps you dislike
A thing in which Allah has placed much good.

[Quran, Al-Nisa (Women), 4:19]

Many men find it confusing and difficult to uphold the rights of their wives when there is interference from the parents or another member of the family. The men become influenced by the criticism and opinions of their own parents towards their wives, which can cause hurt and create disharmony between the spouses.

A wife is entitled to live in a dwelling that is safe for her, in a dignified and respectful manner. A husband cannot keep a wife to be treated unjustly by himself, his parents or anyone else. Any practice that leads to injustice is unacceptable upon religious and moral grounds. There must be stability, security, justice and peace in Muslim homes where rights are to be protected.

Allah Almighty says:

> Let not your enmity for anyone lead you into the sin of
> deviating from justice;
> Always be just: that is being closest to being God-fearing.
>
> [Quran, Al-Ma'idah (The Feast), 5:8]

Parents are entitled to respect and kindness from their children. Sons have a duty to ensure their parents' needs are fulfilled (such as food, clothing, home maintenance), and they are visited from time-to-time to receive companionship.

At the same time however, out of love and kindness, the parents should be prevented from oppressing another human being and committing sins which displease Allah Almighty.

The Messenger of Allah (peace be upon him) said:

> 'Help your brother whether he is an oppressor or an oppressed one.' People asked, 'O Messenger of Allah! It is all right to help him if he is oppressed, but how should we help him if he is an oppressor?' The Prophet said, 'By preventing him from oppressing others.'
>
> [Al-Bukhari]

SLANDERING, BACKBITING AND CURSING

A parent may directly advise a daughter-in-law in kindness on an issue they may have concern about, but the husband's parent should never say anything bad about the daughter-in-law to her husband or to anyone else.

Allah Almighty says:

> O you who believe!
> Shun much suspicion; for lo! Some suspicion is a crime.
> And spy not, neither backbite one another.
> Would any of you like to eat the flesh of his dead brother?
> You abhor that (so abhor the other)!
> And keep your duty to Allah.
> Lo! Allah is Relenting, Merciful.
>
> [Quran, Al-Hujurat (The Private Rooms), 49:12]

Slandering, backbiting and cursing are major sins. Any person causing a break-up of a husband and wife's relationship has committed a violation to such an extent that this person falls to the level of Satan.

If a parent-in-law has given advice to their daughter-in-law, then it is the daughter-in-law's decision to follow their advice or not. A daughter-in-law has no religious obligation to obey the in-laws, and she must not be forced to obey them as this will lead to oppression.

There are no ties of kinship between a parent and their daughter in- law and a parent and their son-in-law. The parents have rights over their own children, whom they raised, but a parent has no rights over a daughter-in-law and a son-in-law.

Parents should not give the daughter-in-law orders directly or indirectly by way of manipulating their son. However, they may advise her with compassion, and then it is her own choice whether to follow their advice or not. Every human being is accountable to Allah Almighty only for their own actions and deeds.

Good behaviour and kind treatment towards young, old and fellow humans is part of a Muslim's character.

The Messenger of Allah (peace be upon him) said:

He does not belong to us [Muslims] who is not kind to our young and does not respect our old.

[Al-Tirmidhi]

IS THE LABOUR OF A DAUGHTER-IN-LAW FREE?

Many South Asian mothers-in-law do not like their daughters-in-law to take over and run the affairs of the husband's home, yet they are very happy for them to do the domestic chores under their control, not as a mistress of the husband's house but as a servant. Mothers-in- law like to think they have the right to rule and mould a daughter-in- law's personality only because she happens to be married to their son.

The mother-in-law cannot have the same tender, motherly love and emotions towards her son's wife as she does for her own children whom she raised from childbirth. She may not treat her son's wife in the same affectionate manner, appreciating her and overlooking her faults as she would with her own children. She will have far greater expectations from her son's wife than from her own daughter. Allah Almighty has not placed on a daughter-in-law's shoulders an almost impossible burden of trying to please someone who proves to be too difficult to please. In reality, there are very few mothers-in-law who treat their daughter-in-law as they would their own daughter.

Allah Almighty says:

> Verily the most honourable of you near Allah is that (believer) who has *taqwa* (is God-fearing and has righteousness) and loves Allah much.
>
> [Quran, Al-Hujurat (The Private Rooms), 49:13]

Only Allah is the best judge of a person's heart and condition and knows who the superior person is.

A man would not appreciate a harassing, discriminating,

dictatorial and jealous boss being around him twenty-four hours a day, seven days a week. Nor would he appreciate being commanded on a daily basis on how he must run his affairs, how he must dress, when and how much to eat, what chores he must complete today, how he must entertain the guests, what to cook and prepare for them, and so forth.

This is what many South Asian daughters-in-law have to tolerate day after day after day. Human beings become slaves, suppressed and moulded by others, whether they are men or women, if they are not allowed to use their intellect and education, nor express their views, opinions, ideas, emotions and feelings.

For the South Asian Muslim community, to say that the wife is obliged to serve and take care of the husband's parents is only a cultural statement. From the Islamic perspective, it is a totally false statement. It is these false teachings used in the name of Islam that lead to injustices and oppression within homes.

Islam does not place on the shoulders of a daughter-in-law any such legal obligation or responsibility. In fact, the daughter-in-law has the right to ask for compensation for the work.

A wife already has a great responsibility in running the affairs of her home, and raising her children in a correct manner in accordance with Islamic guidance. It is this responsibility that she will be held accountable for.

This Indian concept of the wife 'marrying the family' has absolutely no basis in Islamic law. The two families of the husband and wife become related to one another through the marriage of their children.

The dominance, interference and control exerted by many mothers-in-law often cause the daughters-in-law misery, insecurities and inferiority complexes. This oppressive environment creates a negative attitude within the daughter-in-law, and she can develop bitter feelings towards her husband who has failed to protect her.

In turn, the husband feels his wife's resentment towards him and his parents, which makes him think she is at fault. Consequently, the aggravation and misery experienced by the spouses, and their cold, bitter and spiteful feelings towards each other, seep through their own marital relationship and influence the mentality, welfare and upbringing of their children.

Our research shows that it is mainly the Asians from the Indian subcontinent who have this cultural practice of living in a joint family system. A woman living with her husband's family is the cultural norm amongst Hindus, Sikhs and Muslims in the Indian subcontinent. A wife in India is given no choice in the matter. However, Islam gave the Muslim wife a divine right to live in tranquillity with her own husband over 1400 years ago.

EXAMPLES OF COMMON SITUATIONS IN SOUTH ASIAN FAMILIES AND WHAT ISLAM SAYS

Here are some typical examples of the many cases that take place within South Asian households. We have outlined what Islam says in regard to these situations.

Example 1
After nine months of pregnancy, a woman gives birth to her child. Her husband's parents immediately name the child without seeking permission from the baby's mother. The husband decides to please his parents and not uphold his wife's right, so she has no say in the naming of her own child to whom she had given birth.

The mother's right has been violated. There must be mutual consultation between the mother and the father to name their baby. The baby's right upon the parents is to give it a name with a beautiful meaning. The husband must fear Allah Almighty and should not oppress his wife to please his parents. The husband and his parents have oppressed a human being and all three have committed wrong.

Allah does not forgive the deeds of people who have violated rights of others, unless forgiveness can be obtained from the person oppressed.

The Messenger of Allah (peace be upon him) stated:

> On the Day of Judgement, rights will be given to those to
> whom they are due (and wrongs will be redressed)...
> [Muslim]

> Whoever is guilty of doing some wrong against a fellow human
> being, whether in regard to his honour or anything else, he
> should obtain his forgiveness before the Day of Judgement,
> when there will be no money to pay for it. If he has any good
> deeds they will be taken away from him to the extent of his
> wrongdoing. And if he has no good deeds, the sins of the wrong
> one will be taken and put on him.
> [Al-Bukhari]

Example 2
A mother-in-law returns home to find that the food has been burnt.
She calls her daughter-in-law and tells her off. The daughter-in-law
confesses to the mother-in-law that her husband called her over to
him so she went. The mother-in-law blames the daughter-in-law for
seducing her son and rebukes her for having sexual relations with
him during the day. This news comes out of the house and spreads
quickly across the neighbourhood and their village.

According to the *shariah*, the wife has a right to exclusive, total privacy in her home so no-one can enter upon her without her permission. At the same time, she must not allow anyone into the house of whom her husband disapproves. No-one has the right to know of any secrets or intimate details of the spouses.

In accordance with the *shariah*, the mother-in-law has no legal rights over the daughter-in-law. The mother-in-law has no right to harass the daughter-in-law or tell her off for burning the food. The daughter-in-law is under no obligation to cook for the in-laws and if she was cooking, the mother-in-law should show gratitude for this as it is a charitable deed; she should make *duaa* (supplications) to Allah Almighty for her daughter-in-law for cooking her food.

It should not have been necessary for the daughter-in-law to divulge any secret of herself and her husband, as this is an intrusion of the utmost secrecy and privacy between spouses. The mother-in-law was in no position to accuse her daughter-in-law of seducing her son, as the wife has a duty to go to her husband if he asks, even if it is the daytime.

The Messenger of Allah (peace be upon him) said:

> When a man invites his wife for his sexual need, she should go to him even if she was working at the outdoor oven.
>
> [An-Nasai, Ahmad]

Questions one may ask:

- Why does the daughter-in-law not have her exclusive right to her home and privacy without any interference or intrusion from the mother-in-law?
- Who told the neighbours of what happened?

The Quran commands that the husband and wife must live in secrecy, privacy, and confidentiality. Their intimacy must not be revealed or exposed to others as Allah Almighty has described a husband and wife's relationship to be as close and concealing of each other's secrets as clothing is to a body.

Allah Almighty says:

> They are garments for you and you are garments for them.
>
> [Quran, Al-Baqara (The Cow), 2:187]

Example 3

A woman gives birth to a female child, and in some village communities her in-laws reduce the mother's food and blame her for giving birth to a baby girl instead of a baby boy.

During a wife's pregnancy and the suckling period, the Quran commands that the husband takes extra good care of his wife, and be extra supportive to her in terms of her food and nourishment. A mother needs better food and nourishment when she is pregnant, so she can produce a healthy baby; and also when she is breastfeeding so that she has an adequate supply of milk. The nutrients and nourishment from the mother are passed on to the child. The husband should pay the wife compensation for suckling their child.

Allah Almighty says:

> And if they are pregnant,
> Then spend your substance on them
> Until they deliver (the baby):
> And if they suckle your child,
> Give them recompense:
> And take mutual counsel together,
> According to what is just and reasonable.
> [Quran, Al-Talaq (Divorce), 65:6]

In accordance with the Quranic verses, a mother's food and nourishment should have improved during pregnancy and breastfeeding, not reduced, and compensation should be paid to her whilst she is breastfeeding.

The Messenger of Allah (peace be upon him) told the men in the *hadith* narrated by Jabir:

> They (women) have a right on you – that you provide them
> with food and clothing in a fitting manner.
> [Muslim and Abu Dawud]

Science has proven that it is not the baby's mother, but the baby's father's sperm that determines the gender of their child, although of course the father has no choice in this matter.

In the female, there are two sex chromosomes which are called the XX chromosomes and which do not change. In the male, the two chromosomes are different: there is the X chromosome, which corresponds with the female chromosome, and the Y chromosome. The man has XY chromosomes and the woman has XX chromosomes. If an X chromosome from the man fertilises the woman's ovum, this will develop into a girl. If a Y chromosome from the man fertilises the ovum of the woman, this will form a boy. The gender of the baby's sex is determined by the father's chromosomes and not by the mother.

THE IMPLICATIONS OF JOINT FAMILY CULTURE

In India, the sons would bring their wives to live with their parents in one house. In Hindu culture, the house or property of the parents is passed down to the sons after their death and their own daughters receive no inheritance from their father. At a Hindu wedding, the daughter receives *jehaiz* (wealth) from her parents, as she has no claim of any inheritance.

In many South Asian Muslim communities, as the bride enters the in-laws' house, there are very high expectations of a generous *jehaiz* from the bride's parents such as electrical goods, household furnishings, crockery, china, utensils, jewellery (gold or silver), or clothes with accessories. Presents are expected for the bridegroom, his immediate family and his extended family members, and the list goes on. Sometimes there is also pressure upon the bride's own brothers, if they are earning, to contribute towards the *jehaiz* for their sister's marriage. Although some daughters-in-law are happy to live with the husband's parents because they have good mutual understanding and she is treated with love and affection, these cases are rare.

Here are many of the disadvantages that we have discovered for the brides who live within the in-laws' household:

1. Sons and daughters are not given their full right to education in accordance with Islamic teachings, because the father is spending money on accumulating his daughter's *jehaiz* for her wedding, rather than investing it in their education.

2. The bride's father is under tremendous financial pressure to give *jehaiz* to please the daughter's future in-laws.

3. Many South Asian fathers have been known to go as far as accepting bribery, or accumulating *jehaiz* through other unlawful means, with the result they go into debt to try and meet the expectations of their daughter's future in-laws.

4. Many poor fathers, if they have more than one daughter, end up with lifelong debts in trying to obtain sufficient *jehaiz* for their daughters' marriages, causing ill health.

5. The bride's parents feel obliged to give extravagant *jehaiz* to please the husband's family, because if they do not, their daughter will receive harsh and abusive treatment at the hands of the in-laws. The in-laws would harass their daughter, mocking the cheap gifts that have been given.

6. If a bridegroom gives some *mahr* to the wife at the marriage, the man's mother expects many times more in return.

7. Display of *jehaiz* is made to meet the demands, greed and expectations of the families, and in order to gain a higher and more honourable status.

8. In some South Asian communities, there are competitions on making a display of *jehaiz*. The guests at

the wedding are invited to view, inspect and discuss the *jehaiz*, leading to materialistic competitions for future displays of *jehaiz*.

9. Much time, effort and energy is wasted upon bickering, disputes, and competing with one another to attain wealth to show off during these ceremonial times.

10. Remarks, boasting, and abusive comments are often made, and one hears competing remarks such as, 'We gave this to them but so-and-so didn't give that to us.' These competing remarks are common especially after the *jehaiz* has been displayed at weddings, leading to backbiting, slander and harassment.

11. The daughter-in-law, being the outsider, is placed under tremendous pressure to obey the whole of the household in performing whatever tasks they demand from her. Instead of becoming a wife for the husband and the 'mistress of her husband's house' in accordance with the *shariah*, she ends up becoming a slave or servant for the husband's family.

12. If she disobeys the husband's parents or his siblings, she is criticised, abused, treated harshly, and left unfed, whilst complaints are made to her parents of her rudeness and disobedience.

13. Many wives living with their husbands are harassed, abused and demoralised by their in-laws, as though these women can never be good enough for their sons. These young wives suffer in an inhumane and demeaning way, as they are frequently made to feel inferior to the husband and his family.

14. There is frequently gossip and backbiting with families all living together.

15. Living together in one house can, and does, lead to lasting quarrels and broken ties over money and inheritance. When the parents die, families who have lived together, and thus put all their income into one home, struggle to distinguish what belongs to whom, which leads to sour relations.

The Messenger of Allah (peace be upon him) has very strictly prohibited a wife's brother-in-law from even entering any of their living quarters when they are alone to avoid wickedness. There is a very strong prohibition for a man to be living in the same dwelling as his brother's wife.

The Messenger of Allah (peace be upon him) said:

> 'Beware of entering upon women.' A man asked, 'O Messenger of Allah, what about the brother in-law?'
> He (peace be upon him) said, 'The in-law is death.'
> [Al-Bukhari and Muslim]

Brothers should live separately with their own wives and children. If they cannot afford their own separate houses, the brothers should divide a house into separate quarters or buy separate apartments for their own individual families and live in accordance with the teachings of the *shariah*. It is strongly prohibited for one brother to be living with the wife of another brother in the same home, as such an act can lead to infidelity.

Brothers who live separately with their own families bring respect, privacy and dignity into each other's homes and livelihoods, which is better morally and materialistically. This clean, dignified and honourable way of living prevents ties of kin being broken over inheritance. It makes it easier for the sons and the daughters to receive their appropriate share of inheritance from their father's wealth and property.

The teachings of the *sunnah* show us how to live our lives. The Messenger of Allah (peace be upon him) did not send his daughters to live in a house with their in-laws.

Today's typical South Asian Muslim marriages have become a materialistic competition of greed, selfishness, pride and arrogance. They result in oppression, misery, and corruption, and contribute to the failure of the nation's economy as a whole.

Amidst such a corrupt and greedy culture, the great need to address and resolve real and serious life issues, such as education, health, homelessness, poverty, crime, drugs, employment and the welfare of society, is all too neglected.

CONTRIBUTING AND BENEFITING THE LOCAL COMMUNITY

The wives of the Messenger of Allah (peace be upon him), such as Aisha bint Abu Bakr, Saffiya and Umm Salamah (may Allah be pleased with them), proved to be great scholars and taught others. Aisha bint Abu Bakr would even teach and correct the *sahaba* (companions) of the Messenger of Allah (peace be upon him). One of Aisha's students, Urwah ibn al-Zubayr, states as recorded in *Tadhkirah al Huffaz*:

'I did not see a greater scholar than Aisha in the learning of the Quran, obligatory duties, lawful and unlawful matters, poetry and literature, Arab history and genealogy.'
The women of Ansar asked the Messenger of Allah (peace be upon him) to appoint a special day for them so they could learn from him, which he (peace be upon him) arranged once a week. The women were free to ask questions of a personal nature to understand their religion properly. Aisha (may Allah be pleased with her) said, 'How good are the women of Ansar! Shyness did not prevent them from understanding their religion properly.'
[Muslim]

Aisha (may Allah be pleased with her) cared for the orphans and poor children. Through her education and guidance, some of them became great scholars. It happens comparatively often in South Asian Muslim households that if a husband allows his wife to do some charitable work that may benefit society, the wife's in-laws are keen to interfere and undermine his decision. For example, if the husband has given permission to his wife to utilise her knowledge and skills in teaching, she faces huge opposition from the in-laws. The husband's parents prefer their daughter-in-law to stay in the house under their dominance, where she can continue to serve them and entertain their guests.

The society of the Indian subcontinent places much cultural pressure and expectation on sons with regard to what they must do for their parents and how they should live their lives, incorrectly using Islam as its defence. Undoubtedly, parents should be treated with the utmost respect and kindness, but even they cannot go against the commands of Allah Almighty.

If the parents are capable of supporting themselves, then they should strive to work for as long as possible and not depend on their sons or anyone else unnecessarily. Fathers should not make themselves intentionally unemployed just because their sons have started earning, but should continue to work, earn their own living and give *sadaqa* from their own income, for as long as they are able to do so. Islam encourages a productive, independent and healthy society. Work and training is good for the mind, body and soul. Righteous work increases a person's good deeds and erases many sins. One should aim to accumulate good deeds in this world as much as possible to reap its rewards in the Hereafter.

Allah Almighty says:

> Those who believe and work
> Righteous deeds – from them
> Shall We blot out all evil
> (That may be) in them,

And We shall reward
Them according to
The best of their deeds.

[Quran, Al-'Ankabut (The Spider), 29:7]

Work, because Allah will observe your work, and his Prophet
and the believers.

[Quran, Al-Tawba (Repentance), 9:105]

8

Joint family culture is not supported by the *sunnah*

The Messenger of Allah (peace be upon him) had six children with Khadija, his first wife (may Allah be pleased with her). Their children were Al-Qasim, Abd-Allah, Zainab, Ruqayya, Umm Kulthum and Fatima (may Allah be pleased with them). He (peace be upon him) later had Ibrahim, through Maria. The sons, Al-Qasim, Abd-Allah, and Ibrahim (may Allah be pleased with them), all died. The daughters, Zainab, Ruqayya, Umm Kulthum, and Fatima (may Allah be pleased with them), survived and married.

The Messenger of Allah's (peace be upon him) eldest daughter, Zainab, married Abu al-'As ibn al-Rabi. His second daughter, Ruqayya, was married to Uthman ibn Affan. After Ruqayya's death, Umm Kulthum was also married to Uthman ibn Affan. Zainab, Ruqayya and Umm Kulthum died during the lifetime of the Messenger of Allah (peace be upon him). The only child that survived till after his death was his youngest daughter, Fatima. She died six months after his death.

At the age of eighteen, Fatima was receiving proposals for her hand in marriage from various men. When Ali ibn Abi Talib (may Allah be pleased with him) came to see the Messenger of Allah (peace be upon him), he appeared to be shy. The Messenger of Allah (peace be upon him) noticed that Ali had something on his mind. The Messenger of Allah (peace be upon him), having realised what Ali was thinking, asked him whether he had come to make a marriage proposal to Fatima. Ali admitted that he had. The Messenger of Allah (peace be upon him)

43

asked Fatima, what she thought of the marriage proposal from Ali. Fatima consented to this marriage proposal. Ali was advised by the Messenger of Allah (peace be upon him) to sell his shield so that he could provide Fatima with a *mahr*. The shield was sold for four hundred dirhams. Fatima's *mahr* was four hundred dirhams. The Messenger of Allah (peace be upon him) married his daughter, Fatima bint Muhammad (may Allah be pleased with her), to Ali ibn Abi Talib (may Allah be pleased with him) in Madina.

The Messenger of Allah (peace be upon him) did not give anything to Ali for the marriage except his *duaa* (supplication). He (peace be upon him) prayed for the couple to have a happy and blessed future. The guests were offered dates and they too prayed for Ali and Fatima at the wedding ceremony.

> Abu Jafar said, 'When the Messenger of Allah came to Madina, he stayed with Abu Ayyub for a year or thereabouts. When Ali married Fatima, He (peace be upon him) said to Ali, 'Look for a house.' Ali looked for a house and found something a little distant from the Prophet (peace be upon him).
>
> [Muhammad Ibn Sa'd, *Women of Madina*, p.15. Publisher: Ta-Ha.]

It was in this house that the marriage of Ali and Fatima was consummated. The Messenger of Allah (peace be upon him) did not send his daughter to live in the household of her in-laws after her marriage. Ali and Fatima lived in their own separate house.

The mother of Ali was called Fatima bint Asad. She had been one of the first women to embrace Islam in its early stages. She was the wife of Abu Talib, who was the Prophet's paternal uncle. He had died in Makkah before the immigration to Madina. As a widow she lived in her own house in Madina. She did not live with her son, Ali, and his wife.

The Messenger of Allah (peace be upon him) did not give any gifts to Ali's mother for the marriage of his daughter to her son. He (peace be upon him) did not give gifts to any of Ali's family members. He (peace be upon him) gave his daughter a few items for her own personal use. There was no display made of any wedding presents for the guests to view. Fatima bint Muhammad set up her new house with some basic items such as a bed, a pillow, plates, glass, a leather water bag, and a grinding stone for grinding flour. In those days there was no running water, gas or electricity in the home. The water was normally brought into the house from the well outside.

The Messenger of Allah (peace be upon him) wanted to see his daughter more often. Therefore Fatima and Ali moved to another house near the Prophet's mosque.

The Messenger of Allah (peace be upon him) would visit Ali's mother, Fatima bint Asad, to enquire about her welfare. She and her husband, Abu Talib had taken care of Muhammad (peace be upon him) when he was an orphan. The Messenger of Allah (peace be upon him) had a great deal of love and respect for Fatima who had looked after him (peace be upon him) as her own child.

When Fatima bint Asad died in Madina, the Messenger of Allah (peace be upon him) went to her house and prayed that Allah Almighty would give her the garments of Paradise. She was wrapped in his shirt before her burial.

The *sunnah* of the Messenger of Allah (peace be upon him) shows and teaches us that he (peace be upon him) did not send his daughter to her in-laws' household after her marriage, but instructed Ali to find a dwelling for his daughter to live in with her husband.

All sons should ensure that their parents receive kind treatment, food, and maintenance, and should visit them from time-to-time for companionship, but Islam does not place an obligatory duty on sons and their wives to live with the parents.

The joint family system was not a practice of the Messenger of Allah (peace be upon him).

Allah Almighty says in the Quran:

> Verily in the Messenger of Allah you have a good example.
>
> [Quran, Al-Ahzab (The Joint Forces), 33:21]

During the life of the Messenger of Allah (peace be upon him),

Arab Muslim women generally went to live with their husbands in their own separate houses, or separate quarters, or a separate apartment from the husband's family members.

The Messenger of Allah (peace be upon him) had more than one wife at one time, and each wife had her own quarters around the courtyard of the mosque with its own separate entrance.

To date, Muslim Arab nations (such as Egypt, Syria, Iraq, Lebanon, and Saudi Arabia), Far Eastern Muslim nations (such as Malaysia and Indonesia), African Muslim nations (such as Sudan), and European Muslim nations (such as Turkey), do not generally practise joint family culture.

Joint family culture is neither from the Quran nor from the *sunnah*. Allah Almighty sent us the perfect role model and example to imitate, follow and obey. It is the *sunnah* of the Messenger of Allah (peace be upon him) that we are to follow: his example, his teachings, his guidance, his sayings and his actions – not the sayings of those who are preaching the continuance of a deep rooted, corrupt culture and its oppressive traditions, by distorting the true principles of Islam.

Allah Almighty commanded the Messenger of Allah (peace be upon him) in the Quran to say:

> If you love Allah, follow me.
> [Quran, Al-Imran (The family of Imran), 3:31]

It is the duty of Muslims to purify their *deen* (religion) and follow the *sunnah* (practice of the Prophet). It is a duty to cleanse the *deen* from cultural practices that distort the reputation and the beauty of true Islam. A cultural practice that has proven to be oppressive and unjust must not be accepted upon religious grounds, and needs to be reformed in accordance with the practice of the *sunnah*.

The Messenger of Allah (peace be upon him) said about purifying the *sunnah*:

> This knowledge will be carried by the trustworthy ones of

every generation – they will expel from it the alteration made by those going beyond bounds, the false claims of the liars, and the false interpretations of the ignorant.

[Ibn 'Adiyy, al-Khatib al Baghdadi, Ibn Asakir, others]

Allah Almighty says:

It is not fitting
For a Believer, man or woman,
When a matter has been decided
By Allah and his Messenger,
To have an option
About their decision:
If any disobeys Allah and his Messenger, he is indeed
On a clearly wrong path.

[Quran, Al-Ahzab (The Joint Forces), 33:36]

9

The wife and her home

The Messenger of Allah (peace be upon him) said:

> Each of you is a shepherd, and each is responsible for those
> under his care. A ruler is a shepherd; a man is the shepherd of
> his family; the woman is the shepherd of her husband's house
> and children. For each of you is a shepherd and each of you is
> responsible for those under his care.
>
> [Al-Bukhari and Muslim]

Both the man and the woman have rights as well as responsibilities.
Apart from financial responsibility, the husband must also provide his wife
and children with education, so that the family continues to receive the
correct guidance and does not go astray. It is only by gaining knowledge
that one becomes aware of the correct etiquette, manners, morals, rights,
responsibilities and method of worship.

Allah Almighty says:

> Save yourselves and your
> Families from a fire
> Whose fuel is people and stones.
>
> [Quran, Al-Tahrim (Prohibition), 66:6]

The wife is responsible for guarding her husband's house,
possessions etc. She uses her intellect, love and care to look after
the husband, their home and their children. The wife respects and
obeys her husband, as long as it is not in disobedience to Allah

Almighty. The wife does not leave her house without her husband's permission, as the husband is responsible for her protection and welfare. The husband should not, however, prevent his wife from visiting her parents, as this could lead to breaking ties between his wife and her parents.

A wife should not allow anyone into the house of whom her husband disapproves. The wife is the mistress of her husband's home and fulfils her duties in the house with joy. She must have a good understanding of her important responsibility as a wife and mother. Abu Hurayrah reported that the Messenger of Allah (peace be upon him) said:

> Every soul of Adam's children is a master. The man is the master of his family, and the woman is the mistress of her home.
> [Ibn us Sunni and Abu Bakr il-Muqri]

The running of a home and the upbringing of the children is in itself a challenging and fulfilling experience for the wife. This responsibility helps the wife to establish and contribute towards an organised and productive household, and, in turn, a progressive society. Just as it is for a man to organise his work using his own intellect, the same principle applies to the woman. While their working roles are different, when both the husband and the wife's roles are combined, it creates a secure family unit.

To allow for the smooth running of the home, the wife has the right to be consulted by the husband before he makes a final decision upon their home or family.

> It is a fact, however, that sound administration within the domestic field is impossible without a unified policy. For this reason, the *shariah* requires a man, as head of the family, to consult with his family and then to have the final say in decisions concerning it. In doing so, he must not abuse his

prerogative to cause any injury to his wife. Any transgression of this principle involves the risk of losing the favour of Allah, because his wife is not his subordinate, but she is – to use the words of the Prophet (peace be upon him) – 'the queen of her house,' and this is the position a true believer is expected to give to his wife.

[Abd Ar-Rahman I. Doi, Women in Shari'ah, p.10 Publisher: Ta-Ha.]

Islam highly recommends mutual consultation. In any organisation, communication skills are necessary to achieve successful outcomes. With regards to a husband and wife, consulting and discussing issues improves communication and builds trust, thus making the relationship more fruitful.

Allah Almighty says:

... And take mutual counsel
Together, according to
What is just and reasonable.
[Quran, Al-Talaq (Divorce), 65:6]ng

Good communication finds solutions to many issues. It helps to find compromises. It helps to satisfy the needs of both spouses and resolves problems amicably. Furthermore, good communication establishes a trusting and sincere relationship.

When young wives start learning to manage their own affairs within the home, they acquire essential organisational skills. These skills need to be attained by women early on, when their minds are still quick to learn and develop. Failure to give them their marital rights adversely affects the welfare, progress and economy of the whole nation.

Many South Asian young men and women are often taught by those who are themselves ignorant and need to be educated. Islamic teachings have been distorted to suit ongoing oppressive traditions, handed down from generation to generation. As a consequence, many distance themselves from Islam because they have been oppressed in the name of Islam.

When in fact it is the traditional cultural practices that suppress them, while Islam liberates them.

Women represent a large portion of the population. Women are the mothers and teachers to their sons and daughters, producing entire next generations. When young wives are not given the opportunity to manage their own homes or benefit the community, their minds wander elsewhere for an outlet. These outlets are often the bazaar, idle talk, gossip, frequent unnecessary socialising, and competing in materialism.

The main education that is passed to many South Asian Muslim women is how to live under the domain of another woman, who herself is often ignorant and in need of much education. Therefore much time and energy is drained within the homes in competing in issues that have no importance and do not benefit the community. Unfortunately it is oppression, materialism and corruption that are passed down to much of the next generation, because within the homes children are learning from the elders. Instead of competing in attaining good deeds and being concerned about their eternal lives in the Hereafter, many South Asian women are obsessed about attaining pride through their sons and competing in materialism.

Allah Almighty says:

> It is not your wealth
> Nor your sons, that will
> Bring you nearer to Us
> But only those who believe and work
> Righteousness – these are
> The ones for whom there is
> A multiplied reward.
> [Quran, Saba' (Sheba), 34:37

10

Obedience to parents and justice

Allah Almighty says:

We have enjoined on man
(To be good) to his parents
In travail upon travail
Did his mother bear him,
And his weaning is in two years:
Show gratitude to Me
And to your parents:
To Me is (your final) Goal.
But if they strive
To make you join
In worship with Me
Things of which you have
No knowledge, obey them not.

[Quran, Luqman (Luqman), 31:14–15]

Allah Almighty tells us about the rights of the parents. The Quran emphasises respect and kindness towards parents – parents who nourish and care for their child through its childhood. The mother has played an important role as the child-bearer and in return the child must show kindness, respect, and obedience.

The Quran goes on to remind us there is no greater authority than Allah Almighty, and believing in one God means obeying only Him. When a human being obeys other than God, it is in contradiction with the commands of Allah Almighty. When a human being disobeys Allah's order and obeys the command of someone else, the human being is associating partners with Allah Almighty. If there should be conflict between Allah's command and the parent's order, the children have an obligatory duty to is obey the parent's order and to obey only Allah's command.

The Messenger of Allah (peace be upon him) said:

> There is no obedience to the creation if it involves disobedience
> to the Creator.
> [Ahmad]

Another *hadith* narrated by Ali (may Allah be pleased with him) states that the Messenger of Allah (peace be upon him) said:

> Obedience may not be offered to a human being if it involves
> disobeying Allah. Obedience should only be in good things.
> [Al-Bukhari, Muslim]

With reference to South Asian joint family culture, if the daughter-in-law insists on having a separate dwelling from the husband's family members, then it is the duty of the husband to fulfil his wife's compulsory right according to the *shariah*.

If the parents demand that she live with them, then her husband must disobey his parents in this matter. The husband does not have to give his wife a separate house if he cannot afford to do so, but he must give his wife at least a portion of the house, such as separate quarters, that is exclusively hers. The wife should be able to bring up her children peacefully in the privacy of her own home.

When the wife and the in-laws are living apart from one another, it puts the man in a better position to fulfil his obligations towards the wife and parents. A husband must not oppress his wife to please his parents, nor must he break his relationship with his parents. A man must be just in all his dealings.

Allah Almighty says:

O you who believe!
Stand out firmly
For justice, as witnesses
To God, even as against
Yourselves, or your parents,
Or your kin, and whether
It be (against) rich or poor;
For God's claim takes precedence over both.
[Quran, Al-Nisa (Women), 4:135]

The husband's parents cannot intrude upon their son's wife or go through her personal possessions, as many South Asian mothers-in-law do, thinking it is their right just because she is married to their son. This mentality has no basis in Islam and goes totally against the teachings of the Quran and the *sunnah*.

A Muslim home must acquire peace, privacy, security and tranquillity and therefore it is not allowed that anyone enter someone else's home without seeking permission first, let alone go into their bedroom or search through their personal possessions.

The Messenger of Allah (peace be upon him) did not enter anyone's home including his own children's without first seeking permission. If parents become angry with their sons for disobeying them by not forcing their wives to live with them, their anger is directed not at their sons, but in fact at the command of Allah Almighty.

Allah Almighty says:

Lodge them (wives) according to what you reside out of your means,
Do not harass them in order to make life difficult for them.
[Quran, Al-Talaq (Divorce), 65:6]

It is the responsibility of Muslims everywhere to reform and rid their communities of an ignorant culture that causes injustice in their homes, society and community. With any reform, it means first reflecting and changing yourself and your family, and then striving to spread the goodness to others.

Allah Almighty says:

> Let not your enmity for anyone lead you into the sin of
> deviating from justice;
> Always be just: that is being closest to being God-fearing.
>
> [Quran, Al-Ma'ida (The Feast), 5:8]

11

Obligations to elderly parents and a wife

The Messenger of Allah (peace be upon him) emphasised upon the Muslims, young or old, who had the ability, to strive to be independent. He (peace be upon him) encouraged believers to work and support themselves and their wives for as long as they have the ability to do so, and not to depend on others unnecessarily.

We see that wherever people work and strive, they produce resources and new opportunities. The pioneering culture of a nation produces a prosperous economy. The Messenger of Allah (peace be upon him) was forty years old when he became a Prophet. He (peace be upon him) was a husband, a guide, and a leader of an army, and strived to spread the message of Islam throughout his life. He (peace be upon him) worked tirelessly until the very end of his life when he died in his wife's arms.

The Messenger of Allah (peace be upon him) said:

> Know that the best food is that which comes from your own
> hands.
> [Al-Bukhari]

When all lawful channels of becoming independent and self-sufficient have been exhausted, the believer should then ask for help from another person.

Allah Almighty says:

Work, because Allah, will observe your work
And His prophet and the believers.

[Quran, Al-Tawba (Repentance), 9:105]

Islam encourages the believers to share knowledge and skills, so that they spread goodness to others for the benefit of society, thereby accumulating good deeds for themselves.

If the husband and wife are no longer self-sufficient and have become dependent, it becomes incumbent upon their children to take care of their needs.

The famous 13th century scholar, Shaikh Al-Islam Ibn Taimiyyah, was once asked about a man who was struck by poverty without the means to support his wife and children, but had a wealthy son. Was it permissible for his wealthy son to support his father, stepmother and siblings? Ibn Taimiyyah answered:

> All thanks and praises are due to Allah. In this case, the son is required to spend from his wealth on his father, stepmother and young brothers and sisters. Rather, if he does not spend, he will be committing 'Uquq [hurting one's parents immensely] against his father, cutting the relation of the womb and earning Allah's punishment in this life and the Hereafter. Allah has the best knowledge.
>
> [Majmu Al-Fatawa, vol. 34, p. 101]

If the parents have become homeless and cannot afford to accommodate themselves, it becomes an obligation upon their sons to provide them with a dwelling within their means. If the parents have become physically dependent or reached an old age, it becomes an obligation upon their son for the parents to live with him, so that they can be cared for.

When the dependent old parents are living with their son, it is the duty of their son to fulfil the obligations towards the parents without subjecting his wife to any harassment from them. The daughter-in-law would not feel inclined to care for her husband's parents if they have been unkind or unjust towards her.

However a wife may wish to take this opportunity, with the intention of gaining reward from her Lord, to help the husband's parents during this difficult, dependent old age. The husband still has the obligatory conjugal duties towards his wife, such as treating her kindly and upholding her rights. He must protect and defend his wife even if someone talks badly about her behind her back. The husband must not pressurise his wife to take care of his parents, as this is his obligation (because they raised him) not hers.

For a child to take care of his own elderly parents is the best deed. Zurah bin Ibrahim said that a man came to Umar (may Allah be pleased with him) and said:

> 'I have an old mother who is unable to answer the call of nature, so I carry her on my back. I also help her perform ablution while turning my face away from her (out of respect). Have I fulfilled my duty towards her?' Umar (may Allah be pleased with him) said, 'No.' 'Even though I carry her on my back and exert myself in her service?' Umar said; 'She used to do the same for you when you were young while hoping that you will live, whereas you wait for the time she will go away (die).'
>
> [Majmu Al-Fatawa, vol. 34, p. 101]

The son can employ someone to assist him to look after his parents if he cannot do it himself. The general South Asian cultural habit of men being undomesticated is not from the *sunnah* of the Messenger of Allah (peace be upon him), as he and other male companions did help in the household chores when time allowed them to do so.

When Aisha (may Allah be pleased with her) was asked:

> 'What did the Messenger of Allah (peace be upon him) do at home?' She replied: 'He acted like other men; he would mend his clothes; milk his goat, and serve himself.'
>
> [Al-Bukhari, Ahmad]

South Asian parents should bring up their sons to be domesticated and helpful, as was the Messenger of Allah (peace be upon him), who was always humble. When boys grow up into men, they should not feel that taking care of their elderly parents is too low an act or beneath them. The children should pray for their parents to receive Allah Almighty's mercy and forgiveness.

However, if the daughter-in-law helps her husband's parents of her own free will, her services and efforts should be appreciated and not criticised.

One of the common complaints made by South Asian wives is that no matter how much they do for their husband's mother she is not satisfied and remains critical towards her daughter-in-law.

The Messenger of Allah (peace be upon him) said:

> Those who do not thank people do not thank Allah.
> [Abu-Dawud]

Some parents insist that their daughter-in-law takes care of them because they do not wish to bother their own child.

The wife has a great responsibility in taking care of her own children, as well taking charge of the affairs of her husband's home. She has a demanding task to ensure that her children receive the correct upbringing, education and guidance so that they grow up to become righteous Muslims.

It is also wrong to believe, as some South Asians do, that the responsibility of taking care of parents lies mainly with the eldest son while their other children have little to do with it. Again this thinking is cultural, whereas in the Islamic context all sons are obliged equally to look after their old, dependent parents. If the sons are earning, they all have financial responsibility within their capacity to spend on their elderly parents. If their daughter is earning and wishes to donate her income towards her parent's needs, it is charity on her part and carries its reward.

Allah Almighty says:

And that you be kind to your parents
If one or both of them reach old age,
Say to them not a word
Of disrespect, nor shout at them
But address them
In terms of honour.
And lower to them the wing
Of humility and say:
'My Lord! Bestow on them
Your Mercy as they did bring me up when I was young.'
[Quran, Al-Isra (The Night Journey), 17:23–24]

12

Education for men and women

Proclaim! In the name of your Lord and Cherisher
Who created – created man
From a clot of congealed blood.
Proclaim! And your Lord is most bountiful.
He who taught the use of knowledge with the pen
Taught man that which he knew not.
[Quran, Al-'Alaq (The Clinging Form), 96:1–5]

Surah al-'Alaq, was the very first revelation to the Messenger of Allah (peace be upon him). It refers to acquiring and teaching knowledge, and spreading Allah Almighty's message.

It is an obligatory duty upon every man and woman to seek knowledge. Allah Almighty has promised a high position to those men and women who have faith and pursue knowledge.

God will
Raise up, to (suitable) ranks
(And degrees), those of you
Who believe and those who have
Been granted knowledge.
[Quran, Al-Mujadala (The Dispute), 58:11]

The Messenger of Allah (peace be upon him) stressed the importance of education for children:

No father can give a better gift to his children than providing
them with good education.

[Al-Bayhaqi]

The Messenger of Allah (peace be upon him) gave special emphasis
to the reward of educating daughters:

'Anyone who looks after and brings up three daughters, or
sisters, educates them well, treats them with compassion, until
Allah makes them self-sufficient, Allah guarantees him Paradise.'
A man asked, 'Suppose there are only two?' The Messenger of Allah
replied, 'Yes, two as well.' The people asked, 'And if there was only
one?' He (peace be upon him) said, 'Yes, even if there is only one.'

[Sharh-al-Sunna]

The parents gain *sadaqa jaria* (ongoing charity) by providing
good education and guidance to their children.

The Messenger of Allah (peace be upon him) said:

When a person dies, all their actions come to an end except
three: ongoing charity, knowledge from which people continue to
benefit and righteous children who pray for them.

[Muslim]

When a mother teaches her children, and a father spends money
and invests in educating the daughters as well, he is also investing in the
education of their grandsons and granddaughters. The daughter will one
day become the mother. She will be the first and foremost teacher of her
children, as the father spends much of his time outdoors. The mother has
a greater responsibility towards the children than the father to ensure
that they are brought up with Islamic morals and character. It is not
difficult to observe that sons and daughters who have educated mothers
make far more progress in all fields than those children whose mothers
are lacking in education.

The parents have a duty to take care of their children by safeguarding their child's health, development and welfare. The correct guidance that the children receive from their parents will help them to become righteous, God-fearing people with good leadership qualities to pass onto their own children.

The character of the Messenger of Allah (peace be upon him) is the perfect role model for all mankind. Allah Almighty has praised the character of our beloved Messenger by saying:

> And you (stand)
> On an exalted standard
> Of character.
>
> [Quran, Al-Qalam (The Pen), 68:3–4]

In order to instil the right values into the children, the mother herself needs to know about the religion of Islam and the life and character of the Messenger of Allah (peace be upon him), in order to use his example to teach herself and her children.

The Messenger of Allah (peace be upon him) was humble, truthful, patient, generous, considerate, forgiving and compassion ate towards other fellow humans.

The Messenger of Allah (peace be upon him) toiled like other men on the battlefields. At the battle of Ahzab, he (peace be upon him) worked to dig the trench along with the other men.

The Messenger of Allah (peace be upon him) was never a male chauvinist. Despite being a great military leader and conveyor of the message of Islam, when he (peace be upon him) was at home, he humbly helped with the domestic chores.

13

Expression of love

My love is obligatory for those who love one another for My
sake.

[Malik, transmitted in Al-Muwatta]

Islam teaches Muslims to love a fellow Muslim sincerely and purely
for the sake of Allah. This sincere love creates purity in people's hearts
and minds. Those people who can achieve this high level of sincere
love will be given an exceptional honour on the Day of Judgement.
Allah Almighty will say to these people:

Where are those who loved one another for My glory? Today
I will shade them in my Shade on the Day when there is no
shade but Mine.
[Muslim]

The expression of love creates unity amongst Muslims. Loving
one another sincerely for Allah's sake is a reminder of equality and
humility amongst Muslim brothers and sisters. Parents should
express equal love towards their sons and daughters. Spouses should
express love and compassion towards one another. Men should
express love for their brothers in Islam, and sisters should express
love for their sisters in Islam. Love should not be kept hidden, but
should be expressed.

The Messenger of Allah (peace be upon him) said:

If a man loves his brother, let him tell him that he loves him.
[Abu Dawud, Al-Tirmidhi]

In another *hadith*, the Messenger of Allah (peace be upon him) said:

> Allah Almighty said: 'Those who love one another for My
> glory will have minbars of light, and the prophets and
> martyrs will wish they had the same.'
> [Al-Tirmidhi]

The Messenger of Allah (peace be upon him) emphasised the importance of expressing love to create a strong and caring society. This environment contributes towards people's attitudes and personalities so that they become selfless, sincere human beings.

Love expressed in words brings sincerity and humbleness into people's hearts and minds. It is often pride and worldly status that gets in the way of expressing one's love towards other fellow human beings.

Anas (may Allah be pleased with him) said that a man was with the Messenger of Allah (peace be upon him), when another man passed by. The first man said:

> 'O Messenger of Allah, indeed I truly love this man.' The
> Messenger of Allah (peace be upon him) asked him, 'Have
> you let him know that?' He said, 'No.' The Messenger of Allah
> (peace be upon him) said, 'Tell him.' He caught up with him
> and told him, 'Truly I love you for the sake of Allah,' and the
> man said, 'May Allah love you who loves me for His sake.'
> [Abu Dawud]

Even if a slave was in the company of the Messenger of Allah (peace be upon him) he was treated in the noblest of ways. The slave would feel that he was in the company of a brother and not in the company of a master. The Messenger of Allah (peace be upon him) would treat his slave with affection, sincerity and as an equal to him. The slave would learn alot and love being in the company of the Messenger of Allah (peace be upon him). This is demonstrated in the example of Zaid ibn Haritha, a slave of the Messenger (peace be upon him), who was given the choice of staying with the Prophet (peace be upon him), or of going freely with his father; he chose to remain with the Messenger of Allah (peace be upon him).

The Messenger of Allah (peace be upon him) taught people to love one another sincerely for Allah's pleasure, for when one loves another for the sake of Allah, the Lord raises the position of the one that loves to being one whom Allah loves.

The Messenger of Allah (peace be upon him) was an example to other men on how to enjoy their wife's company and form a loving bond. Many Muslim couples deprive themselves of the happy and fulfilled marital relationship with which Allah has favoured them. When a husband expresses love to his wife it sheds many sins and is an act of worship.

The Messenger of Allah would joke and play with his wives. He (peace be upon him) raced with his wife Aisha (may Allah be pleased with her) and she won the first race. The Messenger of Allah raced her again on another occasion, and at that time she had put on some weight, and he (peace be upon him) won the race.

Aisha (may Allah be pleased with her) reported that she was with Allah's Messenger during a journey. She said:

> I was not bulky; he told his companions to move forward and
> they did. He then told me: 'come and race me'. I raced him on
> foot and I beat him. But on another journey, when I became
> bulky, he asked me to race him. I raced him and he beat me.
> He started laughing and said: 'This makes up for that beating.'
> [Ahmad, Abu Daawud and others]

The Messenger of Allah (peace be upon him) instructed men to treat their wives with kindness and compassion:

> The best among you is the one who is best towards his family
> and I am the best of you to my family (wives).
> [Al-Tirmidhi]

The love and care between the spouses contributes towards a peaceful, happy and secure environment within their home. This harmonious atmosphere influences the children's personalities in becoming caring, happy, and confident human beings.

Muslims should love one another sincerely for Allah's sake and not for materialistic gain. Many South Asians treat those who have wealth in a great way, but those who do not have wealth are treated in an inferior way. This behaviour is a sign of hypocrisy. This is not love for the sake of Allah Almighty, but for wealth and greed.

The Messenger of Allah (peace be upon him) said:

> You shall not enter Paradise until you have faith and you will
> not have faith until you love one another. Have compassion
> on those who are on the earth, and he who is in Heaven will
> have compassion for you.
> [Al-Bukhari]

A true Muslim will want for his Muslim brother what he likes for himself, regardless of his colour, nationality, race or wealth. A true Muslim will treat others the way he wants others to treat him. A true Muslim will want his fellow Muslims to be successful just as he wishes to be successful.

The Messenger of Allah (peace be upon him) said:

> None of you believes (with true faith) until one loves for his
> brother what he loves for himself.
> [Al-Bukhari and Muslim]

Love is one of the attributes necessary in Islam for a Muslim to enter Paradise.

The Messenger of Allah (peace be upon him) said:

> By the One in whose hand is my soul, you will not enter
> Paradise until you believe, and you will not believe until you

love one another. Shall I not tell you of something that if you do it, you will love one another? Spread peace amongst yourselves.

[Muslim]

14

Inheritance – why a half?

Why does a woman receive half the inheritance of her brother?
Let us look at this example:

> Salim received £6,000 in inheritance money after his father died, therefore his sister, Sadia, in accordance with the shariah, received £3,000. Salim married and gave away £4,000 of mahr to his wife, so he is now left with £2,000 of the inheritance money. Salim will also have the responsibility of working to fully support his wife and their children with his own income. Sadia's inheritance money of £3,000 is exclusively hers; she does not have to share it with anyone.

> A man called Mustafa wants to marry Sadia and gives the mahr of £3,000. Sadia wants the mahr to be paid immediately when the marriage contract is signed. When Sadia marries, she and Mustafa stipulate on their marriage contract for the amount of mahr to be £3,000.

> Sadia received the first £3,000 of inheritance after her father died along with a further £3,000 by mahr through her marriage to Mustafa – a total of £6,000. Mustafa will be responsible for the full financial support and maintenance of his wife, and Sadia will be responsible for taking care of her home and children, but she is not responsible for any financial maintenance. If Sadia should go out to work with her husband's approval, any income Sadia earns will be exclusively hers; she is not obliged to share it with anyone.

A man receives double the inheritance of his sister because he has a financial responsibility towards his wife and children to fully support and maintain them. A woman is given half the inheritance of her brother because the inheritance given to a woman is exclusively hers. No-one has the right to take any of it from her – neither her husband, nor her brother; she can do whatever she pleases with her money.

In reality, it is not always so simple. Some fathers do not leave a will, nor do some of them distribute inheritance in accordance with the commands of Allah Almighty. Some husbands try to get away from giving any *mahr* to their wives. These corrupt practices deny women their many *shariah* rights. Hindu culture denies inheritance to the daughter so a Hindu bride's parents give gifts (*jehaiz*) to their daughter at her wedding, and some South Asian Muslims practise this Hindu custom.

The Messenger of Allah (peace be upon him) stated:

> On the Day of Judgement, rights will be given to those on
> whom they are due (and wrongs will be redressed)...
> [Muslim]

Allah does not forgive the violation of rights, unless forgiveness can be obtained from the person oppressed.

Islam gives a woman half the inheritance proportionate to her brother, but she also receives the *mahr* and full financial support from her husband. The inheritance, *mahr*, and any of her earned income is exclusively hers; she does not have to spend any of it on herself or on her children as that is the financial responsibility of her husband.

Islam gives the woman these rights so that she may gain financial security, dignity, and some economic benefits instead of becoming a totally dependent human being. The wife can go out to work with the permission of her husband because he is responsible for her protection. However, a Muslim woman cannot be forced to go out to work by anyone.

Any income that a woman earns from her own labour is hers and her husband cannot withhold his money just because she is earning or because she has more money than him. The husband is fully responsible for maintenance of his wife and children. If a husband is in genuine need, the wife may provide financial assistance within the household and that is a *sadaqa* for her.

It is wise for a woman to utilise her finances in such a way that she always has some financial security to fall back on should any unforeseen circumstance or tragedy occur. She may think it is useful to keep and rent a property in her own name, or have other small investments that will provide her with some financial security. Some women work hard and use their own money in furnishing and maintaining their husband's home, but if a divorce occurs, they do not always get back what they spent.

Muslims should give equal inheritance to all their sons. Some South Asian Muslim parents give more inheritance to one son than to another, because one was kinder than the other. Although children should be kind and respectful towards their parents, the parents cannot give more inheritance to their favourite child because the law of Allah states how the inheritance must be divided. The parents do not have the right to overrule the commands given by Allah Almighty by passing their own judgements on this matter. Each individual is answerable for their own actions: if a son was rude to his parents, he is accountable for his own actions; if a father did not divide the inheritance in accordance with the *shariah*, he is answerable for his own actions.

Some sons may have financial responsibilities towards other relatives besides a wife and children. If a man's mother does not have a husband to support her, or if the son's parents are poor or too old to support themselves, the son will be obliged to fulfil the parents' needs and necessities.

A man is also responsible for supporting his sister if she does not have a father or a husband to support her. However, sometimes sons are pressurised into providing financial help as well as the dowry at their sister's wedding. It is not the responsibility of the bride's brother, nor the responsibility of her father to provide any form of dowry or financial maintenance. It is the bride's husband who is responsible for providing *mahr* to his wife, as well as full financial maintenance.

Men are also financially responsible for their nieces if they have no father or brother and they are the closest male relatives to them, as well as new sisters who enter Islam and have no-one to support them.

Some South Asian Muslims are in the habit of taking unnecessary advantage of their fellow human beings because they are too lazy to work, or are greedy and cannot bear to see someone else having more than them. This is not the character of a believer. The Messenger of Allah (peace be upon him) strongly encouraged believers to become self-sufficient and not to depend on others unnecessarily.

This limited lifetime on Allah's Earth should be filled with doing righteous deeds for as long as one has the ability to do so.

Allah Almighty says:

> Then shall anyone who
> Has done an atom's weight
> Of good, see it!
> And anyone who Has done an atom's weight
> Of evil, shall see it.
> [Quran, Al-Zalzala (The Earthquake), 99:7–8]

15

Divorce and *khul*

In very exceptional circumstances, if the marriage should fail and there is no longer a possibility for it to continue in peace and harmony, it is better for the couple to part. Divorce must be the final resort, rather than to endure painful, miserable lives together which could be harmful for either one or both of the spouses.

A divorce from a man or a woman is strongly discouraged in Islam, but not prohibited when a marriage has truly become unsuccessful.

The Messenger of Allah (peace be upon him) said:

> Of all things which have been permitted, divorce is the most hated by Allah.
>
> [Abu Dawud]

If there is any chance of reconciliation between the spouses, all efforts should be made to achieve it. If the husband and wife cannot come to a mutual understanding themselves, a male arbiter may be appointed from each side.

Allah Almighty says:

> If you fear a breach between a couple,
> Send an arbiter from his people,
> And an arbiter from her people,
> If the couple desire to put things right,
> Allah will bring reconciliation between them.
>
> [Quran, Al-Nisa (Women), 4:35]

When a man marries, he commissions himself to take full charge in caring for his wife. The wife comes under her husband's protection and support. The husband must show kindness, behave well towards her, respect her rights and treat her in a dignified manner.

Allah Almighty says:

> And they (wives) have taken from you a solemn covenant.
> [Quran, Al-Nisa (Women), 4:21]

Islam teaches people to deal with one another in kindness. If a marriage should resort to a divorce, then the divorce too must take place with kindness and consideration.

Allah Almighty says:

> Then, when they reach the term appointed,
> Either take them back with correctness and courtesy
> Or part with them with correctness and courtesy.
> [Quran, Al-Talaq (Divorce), 65:2]

If the husband definitely cannot fulfil his responsibilities towards his wife, he has clearly been given the easier exit out of the marriage so that he does not harm his wife by keeping her. A wife may release herself from her husband, which is a lesser divorce called *khul*, through the authority of a religious leader such as an official *qazi* (judge) or an official Islamic organisation dealing with Muslim marital affairs. *Khul* will be discussed later in this chapter.

DIVORCE BY THE HUSBAND

If a husband divorces his wife and their marriage had been consummated (sexual intercourse occurred), the husband cannot have any of the *mahr* back and the wife is entitled to keep the full amount.

A divorce by the husband should be pronounced in the presence of two male witnesses so that there is no contradiction, whether the divorce was actually pronounced to the wife or not. However, if the husband pronounced the divorce to his wife without witnesses, it will still count as a pronounced divorce.

Talaq ahsan (most approved divorce) is a revocable divorce and the one that was most approved by the Messenger of Allah (peace be upon him).

This method of divorce gives time and opportunity for the couple to reconcile or unite.

1. When the husband pronounces the divorce, 'I divorce you,' it must be during the state of the wife's purity. In other words, when the wife is not menstruating, so as to ensure that he is not acting due to her inability to engage in sexual intercourse.

2 Once the husband has pronounced the divorce, 'I divorce you,' the wife's *iddah* period, a prescribed waiting period, begins from the first pronouncement. The *iddah* is a certain number of days in which the woman becomes separated from the husband. During the period of *iddah*, she cannot marry another man, nor can she receive a marriage proposal. The restriction of pronouncing the divorce once, gives the husband an opportunity to re-think in case he pronounced it impulsively or in a state of anger. The husband can revoke the divorce by saying, 'I take you back,' during the wife's *iddah* period, which starts from the first pronouncement of the divorce.

3. The husband must abstain from intercourse with his wife after pronouncing the first divorce in her state of purity. *Iddah* for a separated, menstruating woman is three menstrual cycles: the wife has her first period after the divorce is pronounced and becomes pure; she has

75

her second period and becomes pure; she has her third period and as soon as she has performed *ghusl* (bathes) to enter purity for the third time, the waiting period or *iddah* comes to an end. The divorce at this point has become irrevocable and she is now completely divorced. She is free to remarry another man if she wishes to do so.

Allah Almighty says:

And their husbands
Have the better right
To take them back
In that period,
If they wish for reconciliation.
[Quran, Al-Baqara (The Cow), 2:228]

The husband may repent and exercise his right of *raja* (return) to have his wife back during the *iddah* period. If the husband should have sexual relations with her during the *iddah*, the divorce becomes revoked and this would be exercising the right of *raja* (return).

A husband cannot throw his wife out of the house or send her to her parents just because he has pronounced the divorce once. During the *iddah* period, the husband still has an obligatory duty to house his wife in a separate apartment within his house. The husband must provide his wife with full maintenance and living expenses such as food, drink, clothing, etc. until her *iddah* period is complete. If the husband has pronounced divorce once or a second time, has abstained from having sexual intercourse with his wife, and the *iddah* period is complete, the husband loses the right of *raja* and cannot take his wife back. Hanafi jurists say that the husband has the right to take back his wife up to the time of purification after her third menstruation during her *iddah* term, whereas the Maliki and Shafi jurists say that the husband loses the right to have his wife back once the flow of the third menstruation has started.

Once the wife's *iddah* period is complete, the husband cannot remarry his divorced wife unless she marries another man through a legal, binding marriage contract. If the second husband divorces his wife, she should complete the period of *iddah* and then the first husband may propose to her. It is up to her to either accept the proposal or to refuse it.

The prescribed waiting period also allows time for it to be known if the wife is pregnant, so that the lineage of the child is recognised. If the wife is pregnant, the prescribed waiting period for a separated pregnant woman is until she delivers the baby.

If the wife is pregnant, the husband will have added responsibility towards the wife and the child, which is to be discussed in this chapter.

If a woman does not have menstrual cycles, for instance due to her old age, then her waiting period is three months. *Talaq al-bidah* (irrevocable divorce) is a sinful divorce which is either pronounced during the menstrual cycle of the wife, or pronounced three times in one sitting. In the heat of the moment, some thoughtless, arrogant men pronounce divorce three times all at once: 'I divorce you, I divorce you, I divorce you.' This kind of divorce is *Talaq al-bidah*, a forbidden and sinful divorce. It is sinful to pronounce divorce three times in one go as it goes against the *shariah*.

According to the majority of scholars, this divorce is irrevocable. In this divorce, the husband cannot have his wife back afterwards even if he wishes to do so, since the husband has left no opportunity of reconciliation. The divorced wife becomes unlawful for the husband until she has married another man through a legally binding contract who afterwards divorces her. However a minority of the scholars hold the view that the three divorces pronounced in one sitting count as one divorce.

> Since the scholars differ concerning the issue, it is good to look into the circumstances of the man who pronounced the divorces. If he did not intend three divorces by his saying,

77

'You are divorced thrice,' but only to frighten his wife if she did something, then it should be considered only one divorce. For example if he says, 'you are divorced thrice, if you do such and such,' and then she does it, or if he was in a state of extreme anger, or he said three divorces not intending to divorce her completely. Therefore it will be considered as one divorce. If he intends by his saying, 'You are divorced three times,' truly to divorce her thrice and separate her from himself irrevocably so that she may not return to him under any circumstances as the three divorces regulate, then, in this case she will not be lawful for him until she marries another husband. This view is according to the combined understanding between the evidences and a mercy for the Muslim Ummah.

[Abu Bakr Jabir Al-Jaza'iry, Minhaj Al-Muslim, vol. 2, p. 366.

Publisher: Darussalam (http://www.darussalam.com)]

THE REMARRIAGE

Once the husband has divorced his wife completely and it has become irrevocable, he cannot marry his divorced wife unless she has married another man with a correct marriage contract, they have had sexual intercourse, and he has divorced her. The wife divorced by her husband is free to be asked for remarriage after the period of *iddah* is complete.
  Allah Almighty says:

So if a husband divorces his wife
He cannot, after that,
Remarry her until
After she has married
Another husband and
He has divorced her.
[Quran, Al-Baqara (The Cow), 2:230]

Iddah (WAITING PERIOD)

• The *iddah* period for a menstruating woman who is
divorced by her husband, is three menstrual cycles.
• The iddah period of a woman who is not menstruating,
for example due to old age, is three months.
• The *iddah* period for a woman whose husband has
died is four months and ten days.
• A woman's *iddah* period if she is pregnant is until her
baby is born.
• No *iddah* period is prescribed if a woman was divorced
before the marriage was consummated.

MAINTENANCE DURING *Iddah*

Allah Almighty says:

Thus when they fulfil
Their term appointed (*iddah*)
Either take them back
On equitable terms
Or part with them
On equitable terms.
[Quran, Al-Talaq (Divorce), 65:2]

If the husband has pronounced divorce, he is still obliged to treat his
wife in a courteous manner, and continue to provide maintenance until
her *iddah* period is complete. The husband is not allowed to throw her
out of his house or send her off to her father's, brother's or anyone else's
house just because he has pronounced divorce or '*talaq*' once. Such men
act against the injunctions of Islam. The wife is not permitted to leave
her husband's house until her *iddah* period is complete.
Allah Almighty says:

O Prophet, when you
Divorce women,
Divorce them at their
Prescribed periods,
And count (accurately)
Their prescribed periods:
And fear Allah your Lord: and turn them not out
Of their houses, nor shall
They (themselves) leave,
Except in case they are
Guilty of some open lewdness,
Those are the limits set by Allah.
[Quran, Al-Talaq (Divorce), 65:1]

Allah Almighty says:

For divorced women,
Maintenance (should be provided)
On a reasonable (scale).
[Quran, Al-Baqara (The Cow), 2:241]

The husband must maintain the same standard for his wife as he is providing for himself; for example he cannot dress himself like a rich man and have his wife dressed like a beggar.
Allah Almighty says:

Let women in *iddah* live
In the same style as you live
According to your means.
Trouble them not in such a way
As to make things difficult for them
Until they deliver (the baby):
And if they suckle your child
Give them recompense:
And take mutual counsel together,
According to what is just and reasonable.
[Quran, Al-Talaq (Divorce), 65:6]

If the wife is pregnant, apart from providing her with maintenance necessary for daily living, Allah Almighty has imposed on the husband additional duties towards the welfare of the mother and their child. The *iddah* period of a pregnant woman ends when the baby is delivered. However, the father's responsibility of maintaining the child's mother continues during the child's suckling period, which is normally two years. If the mother is not able to suckle the child for two years, they must agree to what is just and reasonable before weaning, and afterwards for what is in the best interest of their child. If the mother is not breastfeeding the child, for example because the milk fails or is insufficient, the responsibility of taking care of the mother still continues with the child's father until the end of the two years' nursing period. They may agree to some other course of feeding the child, such as employing a wet nurse or bottle-feeding, depending on the environment where they are living.

Allah Almighty says:

Mothers shall give suck to their offspring
For two whole years
If the father wishes to complete the term, but he shall bear
the cost of their food
And clothing on equitable terms.
No mother shall be treated unfairly
On account of her child
Nor father on account of his child,
And they shall be chargeable in the same way.
If they both decide on weaning by mutual consent, and after
due consultation,
There is no blame on them, provided you pay (the mother)
what you offered,
On equitable terms,
But fear Allah and know
That Allah sees what you do.
[Quran, Al-Baqara (The Cow), 2:233]

Allah Almighty says:

> In travail upon travail
> Did his mother bear him
> And his weaning is in two years.
> [Quran, Luqman (Luqman). 31:14]

In some exceptional circumstances the period of weaning may be extended.

Allah Almighty says:

> The carrying of the child to his weaning
> Is a period of thirty months.
> [Quran, Al-Ahqaf (The Sand Dunes), 46:15]

The husband should spend upon the mother and their child according to his means. If he is rich, he should spend generously, and if he is poor, he should spend within his capacity.

Allah Almighty says:

> Let the man of means
> Spend according to
> His means, and the man
> Whose resources are restricted,
> Let him spend according
> To what Allah has given him.
> [Quran, Al-Talaq (Divorce), 65:7]

If there was no *iddah* period, a wife who has just conceived or has become pregnant before the divorce was pronounced could have married the very next day or next week. If she did marry soon after a divorce, it would be easy to think that her new husband was the father of her child, whereas it was her previous husband who is the father of that child. The child's own father is the one who is financially responsible for the child, not the stepfather.

Another reason for the period of *iddah* is so that no-one can blame the woman for having committed a sin such as adultery after the divorce, just because she is pregnant.

DIVORCE INSTIGATED BY THE WIFE: *KHUL*

Khul means to liberate from the husband by paying him some compensation. Islam has given the woman an exit to escape from the cruelty of a husband. *Khul* divorce can be asked in exceptional situations, but not without a good reason because the Messenger of Allah (peace be upon him) has said:

> Whichever woman asks for divorce from her husband without any specific reason, the fragrance of Paradise will be unlawful for her.
>
> [Abu Dawud, Al-Tirmidhi]

The *khul* by the wife can be requested on any of the three following conditions:

> (1) That the hatred should be on the wife's part. If the husband dislikes her, he is not eligible to receive compensation from her. Rather he has to be patient with her or divorce her.
> (2) The wife should not demand the marriage separation from him until she reaches a severe level of harm from which she will not be able to maintain the limits (laws) of Allah regarding herself or the rights of her husband.
> (3) The husband should not cause her deliberate harm so that she will separate from him. If he does this, it is not permissible for him to get anything from her as compensation, and he will be a sinner. A *khul* should be considered an irrevocable divorce. If he wants to take her back, she will not be lawful for him except with a new marriage contract.
>
> [Abu Bakr Jabir Al-Jaza'iry, *Minhaj Al-Muslim*, vol. 2, p. 368.
> Publisher: Darussalam (http://www.darussalam.com)]

For the second condition of *khul* above, here are two possible examples when a wife may divorce the husband:

Example A: If a husband loses control, is mentally unstable, influenced by drugs, or has the tendency to cause harm to his wife.

Example B: If the wife has reached a stage whereby she can no longer fulfil the marital obligations towards her husband, and does not go to her husband for sexual relations for good reason if he should call her.

The first *khul* case in Islam is reported by Imam Al-Bukhari:

The wife of Thabit ibn Qais came to the holy Prophet and said, 'O Messenger of Allah, I am not angry with Thabit for his temper or religion, but I am afraid that something may happen to me contrary to Islam, on which account I wish to be separated from him.' The Messenger of Allah (peace be upon him) said, 'Will you give back to Thabit the garden which he gave to you as your settlement?' She said: 'Yes.' Then the Messenger of Allah (peace be upon him) said to Thabit, 'Take your garden and divorce her at once.'

[Al-Bukhari]

The woman felt that she could not observe the laws of Allah and so wanted to be free from the marriage obligations. The Messenger of Allah (peace be upon him) agreed and ordered Thabit to take the compensation for the release of his wife.

Allah Almighty says:

Then there is no blame on either
Of them if she gives back
Something for her freedom.
[Quran, Al-Baqara (The Cow), 2:229]

THREE DIFFERENT METHODS OF DIVORCE
THROUGH *Khul*

1. At the bride's request, *khul* can be stipulated in her marriage contract which allows a woman to dissolve her marriage if her husband agrees to grant her this right. By inserting the stipulation, the husband has authorised the wife to release herself under certain conditions. The husband gives the wife the authority (such as a power of attorney) to pronounce the divorce on his behalf and the wife initiates it.

2. If no stipulation in the contract was made, *khul* can still be demanded in harsh and exceptional circumstances through mutual agreement between the husband and wife. If the wife feels that her husband is not fulfilling his cordial marital obligations towards her, the wife can release herself from him by offering some or all of the *mahr* back that he has given to her, or she can compromise in another way to benefit the husband.

   However the wife need not give more than the *mahr* that she received from her husband to free herself, as we know from the following *hadith*, describing a wife who could not fulfil her obligations towards her husband and wanted a separation from him, even though her husband was not said to be at any fault.

   A woman came to the Messenger of Allah (peace be upon him) and said: 'I hate my husband and would like separation from him.' The Messenger of Allah (peace be upon him) asked, 'Would you return the orchard that he gave you as a dower?' she replied: 'Yes, more than that.' The Messenger of Allah (peace be upon him) said: 'You should not return more than that.' [Al-Baihaqi]

3. If the husband refuses to grant his wife the divorce
    through mutual consent, the woman can free herself
    through the authority of the *qazi*, or imam, or an official
    religious organisation like the *Shariah* Council that deals
    with Muslim marital affairs. In this way, the wife can
    also release herself by paying some or all of the *mahr*
    back to the husband as compensation for her release.
    A woman does not have to have her husband's consent
    for the *khul* divorce despite what some men think. The
    wife can free herself from the marriage by paying some
    compensation to her husband for the *khul* divorce,
    given through the order of an official religious leader
    or an official Islamic organisation dealing in Muslim
    marital affairs at the request of the woman. The official
    religious leader or Islamic organisation will look into
    the allegations that his wife is making to find out if she
    really is unable to live with him. If the *khul* is granted,
    the husband loses the right to reunite with his wife, as
    this is an irrevocable divorce.

NO RETURN OF *MAHR* TO A CRUEL HUSBAND

The husband has been forbidden to treat his wife harshly with the
aim of driving her to divorce him through *khul*, in order that he may
claim back the *mahr*. If the wife is divorcing the husband because of
his cruelty, he forfeits any compensation.
Allah Almighty says:

> Nor should you treat them (women)
> With harshness, that you may
> Take away part of the dower
> You have given them – except
> Where they have been guilty
> Of open lewdness;
> On the contrary live with them

On a footing of kindness and equity.
[Quran, Al-Nisa (Women), 4:19]

If the husband is cruel to his wife, she may not need to forfeit the whole of the *mahr*. The wife can complain to an official *qazi* or the official Islamic organisation, such as the *Shariah* Council, that she wants a *khul* divorce from her husband. The *qazi* or the religious organisation will look into her allegations against her husband, and if the wife is telling the truth, they can tell her husband to repudiate her. If the husband pronounces the divorce, the *iddah* period is three menstrual cycles and she has the right to be maintained by her husband during those cycles of the *iddah* period if she wishes to take this right. As the separation from the husband took place at the wife's request, the *khul* is an irrevocable divorce and the husband does not have the authority to take back his wife during the *iddah* period.

If the husband should refuse to pronounce the divorce, the *qazi* or the *Shariah* Council has the authority to pronounce a *talaq* on behalf of the husband, and she may not forfeit any of the *mahr*. If it is a deferred *mahr*, the husband can become liable for the whole of the *mahr*. If the *qazi* or *Shariah* Council pronounce the divorce and not *khul* on behalf of her husband, the *iddah* period is three menstrual cycles and the wife does not need to return the *mahr*. Again, the husband must also maintain his wife with all her rights during the *iddah* period of the three menstrual cycles, but does not have the authority to take back his wife during the *iddah* period. If the *qazi* or *Shariah* Council pronounce *khul* because they did not find any fault in the husband, the wife will pay back the *mahr* as compensation to free herself from the husband and the *iddah* period is one menstrual cycle. In this *iddah* period of one menstrual cycle, the husband is not responsible for maintaining his wife. The husband does not have the authority to take her back during the *iddah* period of the *khul* divorce as it is irrevocable. *Khul* divorce can also be requested by a girl if she was married before the age of puberty.

When she reaches the age of puberty she has the right to accept or reject the marriage.

After a *khul* divorce, the couple are allowed to remarry again if they should both choose to do so through mutual consent, because the *khul* divorce is instigated by the wife and not the husband.

Many women do not put aside their *mahr*, inheritance, or earned income separately in their own name, which is their exclusive right. A woman should always be aware and make preparations for any unexpected tragedies that may come her way.

Islam gives women the right to buy a home or property in their own name, as well as to rent out a property or make other investments for their own financial security. If a woman earns any income or profit from her own investment, it is hers. Islam gives Muslim women the right to become financially independent and makes it obligatory upon them (and on men) to seek knowledge so they know about their rights and obligations towards others, as well as the *halal* (lawful) and *haram* (unlawful). The women should take their rights given to them by Allah Almighty to become financially secure and confident human beings, instead of feeling helpless and financially dependent.

16

Divorcees and widows encouraged to remarry

Islam gives freedom to widows and divorced women to remarry. Unlike the Hindu religion, which has prevented women from remarrying after the death of their husbands, Islam encourages women to start a fresh life with another man in a noble way.

Allah Almighty says:

If any of you die
And leave widows behind,
They shall wait concerning themselves
Four months and ten days:
When they (widows) have fulfilled
Their term, there is no blame
On you if they dispose
Of themselves in a just
And reasonable manner.
[Quran, Al-Baqara (The Cow), 2:234]

Once a woman has completed her *iddah* period, she is free to consider and accept a proposal of marriage from another man. However if a woman is in her *iddah* period, the man is restricted from making a proposal of marriage until the woman has completed it.

Allah Almighty says:

There is no blame
On you if you make

An offer of betrothal
Or hold it in your hearts.
God knows that you
Cherish them in your hearts:
But do not make a secret contract
With them except in terms
Honourable, nor resolve on the tie
Of marriage till the term
Prescribed is fulfilled
And know that God
Knows what is in your hearts...
[Quran, Al-Baqara (The Cow), 2:235]

The Messenger of Allah (peace be upon him) himself married many widows during his lifetime, and he (peace be upon him) solemnised the marriages of many other widows.

17

The value of time

By (the Token of)
Time (through the Ages)
Verily the human being
Is in a loss,
Except such as have faith
And do righteous deeds
And (join together)
In the mutual teaching
Of truth, and of
Patience and Constancy.

[Quran, Al-Asr (The Declining Day), 103:1–3]

Through time, generations of people have come into the world and passed away. Surah Al-Asr teaches us that a human being will lose against time, except those that have faith, acquire righteous deeds and teach the truth. The time a person spends here on Allah's Earth is restricted, irreplaceable and is so valuable that the *akhira* (Hereafter) depends entirely on it. A human being must learn to value life and time, making every minute count. Once a person's lifespan has terminated, he cannot return to this present human form to correct any matter or to accumulate any further good deed.

Allah Almighty says:

When death comes
To one of them, he says,
'O my Lord, let me return, let me return to life,
In order that I may

Work righteousness in the things
I neglected.' But by no means!
It is but a meaningless word he utters.
[Quran, Al-Mu'minun (The Believers), 23:99–100]

One should make maximum use of one's lifetime on Earth by valuing time, accumulating good deeds, and taking account of oneself for the sake of Allah Almighty.

Umar ibn al-Khattab (may Allah be pleased with him) said about self evaluating oneself before the real test on the Day of Judgement:

Judge yourself before you are judged, evaluate yourself before
you are evaluated and be ready for the greatest investigation.

A person should not only lead a pious life, but also help and guide others to this moral excellence. The person who guides another person to do good deeds earns the same reward as the person who was guided.

The Messenger of Allah (peace be upon him) said:

Whoever guides others to do good will have a reward like that
of the person who does the good deed.
[Muslim]

It is vital to differentiate between the correct guidance and the wrong guidance. There are some people who follow others blindly without thinking for themselves. They do not use their own intellect to judge between right and wrong, and do not research the Quran and the *sunnah*.

One must be careful not to add anything to the religion in the name of Islam, in case it leads to an innovation *(bidah)*. Everyone is responsible and accountable for their own selves and their own actions. One should guide another person to the truth and not falsehood.

Satan will say on the Day of Judgement:

I had no authority over you
Except to call you, but you
Listened to me, so blame not me,
But blame yourselves.

[Quran, Ibrahim (Abraham), 14:22]

The Hereafter is the only everlasting life. Allah Almighty tells men and women to work hard and compete with one another at doing good work and attaining good deeds.

Allah Almighty says:

They enjoin what is right,
And forbid what is wrong,
And compete in doing good,
They are in the ranks
Of the righteous.

[Quran, Al-Imran (The Family of Imran), 3:114]

Allah Almighty says:

It is He who has created death
And life, that He
May try which of you
Is best in deed.

[Quran, Al-Mulk (Control), 67:2]

GIFTS AND CHARITY

People should not be concerned about popularity or status in their community out of arrogance or pride.

Allah Almighty says:

For Allah loves not the arrogant or boastful.

[Quran, Al-Nisa (Women), 4:36]

A gift or *sadaqa* (charity) given to show off to others has no value in the Hereafter. If a gift is given, it should be given with the intention to gain Allah's pleasure. Gifts should not be given with pride, or with the expectation of receiving more generous gifts in return.

Allah Almighty says:

> We have prepared a humiliating punishment
> For those who resist faith
> And those who spend their wealth
> To show off to people, but have no faith
> In Allah and the Last Day.
> [Quran, Al-Nisa (Women), 4:37–38]

The person who gave a gift or did a favour should never remind the person to whom the gift was given of his generosity.

Allah Almighty says:

> Those who spend
> Their wealth in the cause
> Of Allah, and do not follow up their gifts with reminders
> Of their generosity
> Or with injury, for them
> Their reward is with their Lord.
> [Quran, Al-Baqara (The Cow), 2:262]

If someone gives an unexpected gift, it should be considered a blessing, and one should be thankful to Allah Almighty for it no matter how big or small it may be. It is always the thought and intention behind the gift that matters, not its materialistic value.

A charitable donation may be publicised if it encourages others to give as well.

Abu Huraira narrated that a man said to the Messenger of Allah (peace be upon him):

> 'O Messenger of Allah, such and such woman has a reputation
> for engaging very much in prayers, fasting and almsgiving, but

she hurts her neighbours with her tongue quite often.' The Messenger of Allah (peace be upon him) said, 'She will go to Hell.' Then he said, 'O Messenger of Allah, such and such woman engages in only a little prayer (obligatory), fasting and almsgiving and gives just a few pieces of cheese in charity, but she does not hurt her neighbours with her tongue.' The Messenger of Allah (peace be upon him) said, 'She will go to Paradise.'

[Ahmad, Al-Bayhaqi]

The good treatment of our fellow human beings will weigh very heavily on the scales.

The Messenger of Allah (peace be upon him) said:

Nothing will weigh more heavily in the Balance of the believing servant than a good attitude towards others. Verily Allah hates those who utter vile words and obscene speech.

[Al-Tirmidhi]

SELF REFLECTION

Once their children are older, some women spend much time unnecessarily revolving around their grown-up married children, or in unnecessary socialising and gossip.

Allah Almighty says:

Let not your worldly possessions
Or your children make you neglectful
From the remembrance of Allah,
If any act thus, the loss is their own.

[Quran, Al-Munafiqun (The Hypocrites), 63:9–10]

And know
That your possessions and your children
Are but a trial.

[Quran, Al-Anfal (Battle Gains), 8:28]

A believer, male or female, should constantly remind themselves of the purpose of life and accumulate as many good deeds as possible for the *akhira*. They should always seek to purify their intentions and regularly check the sincerity of their deeds.

Allah Almighty says:

> The Day whereon neither
> Wealth nor sons will avail,
> But only he (will prosper)
> That brings to Allah
> A sound heart.
>
> [Quran, Al-Shu'ara (The Poets), 26:88–89]

Allah Almighty prohibits Muslims from becoming proud or arrogant, warning them against such sinful behaviour repeatedly in the Quran.

Allah Almighty says:

> And walk not on the earth
> With conceit and arrogance.
> Of all such things
> This evil is hateful
> In the sight of thy Lord.
>
> [Quran, Al-Isra (The Night Journey), 17:37–38]

Allah instructs the believers to be moderate and humble, and to remember that all our gifts and talents are from Allah Almighty.

Allah Almighty says:

> Successful indeed are the believers,
> Those who humble themselves
> In their prayers;
> Who avoid vain talk
> Who are active in deeds
> Of charity.
>
> [Quran, Al-Muminun (The Believers), 23:1–4]

Allah Almighty says:

> And swell not your cheek
> (For pride) at men
> Nor walk in insolence
> Through the earth
> For Allah loves not any arrogant boaster.
> And be moderate
> In your pace, and lower
> Your voice; for the harshest
> Of sounds without doubt
> Is the braying of the ass.
>
> [Quran, Luqman (Luqman), 31:18–19]

The Messenger of Allah (peace be upon him) said:

> Wise is the one who (continually) assesses himself and performs good deeds for the life after death. And foolish is the one who follows his desires and entertains very high hopes from Allah.
>
> [Al-Tirmidhi]

The Messenger of Allah (peace be upon him) urged the believers to be self-sufficient and independent. When children have grown up or are married, many mothers have more spare time on their hands, but they do not always use it to their own advantage or for the benefit of their local community. How can the extra available time be invested to accumulate good deeds in one's lifetime and even after one's death?
Allah Almighty says:

> Never will I allow to be lost
> The work of any of you
> Be he male or female –
> You are members one of another.
>
> [Quran, Al-Imran (The Family of Imran), 3:195]

97

Start by reflecting and reviewing your own life. This should be done regularly at least once a week. One should take account of one's faults and rectify any wrongs that may have been committed, even if it is only a very small thing such as returning an item of clothing that was borrowed, but not yet returned to its rightful owner. If it is lost, replace it. If that cannot be done, pay for it or compensate for it in another way. If that cannot be done, seek forgiveness from the person from whom it was borrowed. Every deed will be accounted for no matter how great or small.

The Messenger of Allah (peace be upon him) stated:

> On the Day of Judgement, rights will be given to those to
> whom they are due (and wrongs will be redressed)...
> [Muslim]

Reflect upon your character. Strive for a clear conscience and a pure heart. Be considerate, caring, trustworthy, humble, courteous, honest, truthful and reliable. People will sincerely love working with you if they love your character. If people love your character, Allah will love you.

The Messenger of Allah (peace be upon him) said:

> The faith of a man cannot be straight unless his heart
> becomes straight and his heart cannot be straight unless his
> tongue becomes straight.
> [Ahmad]

Any lawful action performed for the sake of Allah is an act of worship. When one intends to earn money lawfully for the sake of Allah it is a good deed; when one spends money lawfully, even to buy food to have the energy for more good work, it is a good deed.

> Actions are judged only by intentions and everyone shall have
> what he intended.
> [Al-Bukhari, Muslim]

Here are more examples of good deeds:

- If a Muslim is doing a paid job or running a business lawfully, with the sincere intention to support himself, his wife and his children, so that the children grow up to become good Muslims, this is an act of worship.
- When one goes to college with the intention of gaining beneficial knowledge, which may serve one's community and gain Allah's pleasure, this is an act of worship.
- When one eats with an intention that the nourishment gained from the food will give one energy to do more work and attain more good deeds, this is an act of worship.
- When a Muslim visits a sick person with the intention to bring some comfort and companionship, this is an act of worship.

The Messenger of Allah (peace be upon him) said:

> No Muslim visits a sick Muslim in the morning but seventy thousand angels will bless him until evening, and if he visits him in the evening, seventy thousand angels will bless him until morning.
> [Al-Tirmidhi]

When one sincerely intends to do a good deed, no matter how simple the action is, in order to gain Allah's pleasure, it is a good deed.

Allah Almighty says:

> Those who believe and work
> Righteous deeds, from them
> Shall We blot out all evil
> (That may be) in them,
> And We shall reward

Them according to
The best of their deeds.
[Quran, Al-Ankabut (The Spider), 29:7]

TIME MANAGEMENT

In order to gain the best use of time, a Muslim needs to analyse the obligations to Allah Almighty, such as: *salah* (prayer), *sawm* (fasting), and Quran reading. A Muslim should be thankful to Allah Almighty for his blessings, make *dhikr* (remembrance), and make *duaa* (supplication) during good and bad times.

A Muslim should reflect on the obligations towards his or her fellow humans, such as:

- Obligations towards the spouse
- Obligations towards parents
- Obligations towards neighbours
- Obligations towards oneself

There may be other obligations towards fellow humans depending on the individual's situation and circumstance.

If spare time is available, a person can consider what skills or knowledge they possess to help serve their community. There is much that women can do even from their own homes.

We are going to give the readers some ideas in this chapter and the following chapter on how a person can maximise their spare time.

It is a good deed to learn or teach any beneficial knowledge, such as can be found in the following: Quran, maths, languages, sciences, computer lessons, cookery, sewing, arts, crafts, or pottery.

To provide ideas on how to benefit the community as well as accumulate continuous good deeds, consider this example:

Faiza taught the Quran with its correct guidance, for the sake of Allah Almighty, to ten students during her lifetime. Faiza had encouraged and guided her students to spread the knowledge that she had taught them. Each of those ten students taught the Quran to eight students (10 × 8 = 80 students) and those eighty students taught the Quran to ten other persons (80 × 10 = 800), so Faiza's knowledge is passed on from generation to generation. Although Faiza has now passed away, she continues to gain reward. This is because Faiza had taken the opportunity in her lifetime to teach others so that her knowledge continues to spread even after her death, and she therefore continues to accumulate good deeds right up to the Day of Judgement.

The Messenger of Allah (peace be upon him) said:

Whoever guides others to do good will have a reward like that of the person who does the good deed.
[Muslim]

Learning and teaching the Quran with correct guidance and understanding is the best deed, whether it is paid or voluntary. A Muslim should not keep knowledge stored up inside, but should share it with others so that they may also benefit from it. By constant learning and the sharing of knowledge, goodness will spread, and all who have learnt and taught will reap their rewards with Allah Almighty.

The spreading of goodness, such as passing on beneficial knowledge or talents, contributes to a motivated and educated society, and a healthy, strong and prosperous nation.

Allah Almighty says:

And do good, that you may prosper.
[Quran, Al-Hajj (The Pilgrimage), 22:77]

18

Volunteering

In this chapter we have given a few ideas on how to utilise spare time effectively, whether it is doing something small or something big. Some people work voluntarily within an organisation. There are great advantages in volunteering. Helping and supporting a charitable organisation can be very fulfilling. The help and support can be given in a variety of ways depending on the needs of the organisation, such as by providing childcare, healthcare, education, training, advice work, administration or any other assistance.

The people helping within the organisation learn new skills for themselves and make new friends. They may also pass on their own ideas, skills and experiences to the organisation, which all contributes in benefiting the community.

When doing something new for the first time, tasks can seem difficult and may not be completed as successfully as you had hoped, but with constant practice and patience, and by gradually gaining confidence, the tasks become easier and more enjoyable. The main difference between an unsuccessful person and a successful person is that the unsuccessful person gives up before he becomes successful. A person should not be discouraged just because someone else may be faster in achieving a similar goal. They should work at a pace they feel confident in. Look at the example of the famous story of the hare and tortoise. Although the hare was faster, in the end it was the persistent tortoise that won the race.

Examples of places where one may find voluntary work are: schools, orphanages, charities, libraries, hospitals, youth clubs and other community organisations.

Ask yourself these questions:

- What organisations are there in my local area relevant to what I wish to do ?
- How much time can I give ?
- Is it convenient for me to work on a regular basis ?

The level of involvement may depend on your time and ability. Even if you can only spare a little time on a regular basis, just think how much this could accumulate to in a year, and how many persons or families you would have helped.

The Prophet (peace be upon him) said:

Do not consider even the smallest good deed as insignificant;
even meeting your brother with a cheerful face is a good deed.
[Muslim]

19

Conclusion

Muslim men and women both have important roles to play in building a fair and just society that adheres to the teachings of Islam. The commands of, and obedience to, Allah Almighty must be the top priority.

Every individual human being is responsible and accountable for his own actions towards another human being.

Allah Almighty says:

> O mankind! Do your duty
> To your Lord, and fear a day
> When no child can absolve the parent,
> Nor can a parent intercede
> On behalf of their child.
> [Quran, Luqman (Luqman), 31:33]

How often do we hear South Asian Muslims themselves talk about the high levels of corruption in their own society and nation? Yet are their children, within their own homes, being brought up where there is no injustice, manipulation or corruption taking place? After all, it is the families that form a community and it is the communities that build the foundation for their society.

Currently information provided about family and marriage in the South Asian Muslim communities tends to be imbalanced. For example, you often hear the community leaders emphasise women's obedience to their husbands but the men's responsibility in providing their wives with maintenance and protection, mentioned beforehand in the same paragraph of the Quran (Al-Nisa, 4:34), is frequently neglected.

It is important to emphasise and educate people concerning the rights of both the husband and the wife, as ignoring the wife's rights can cause her to suffer abuse, torture and interference within the home from other members of the family. In extreme cases, this pattern leads to her being thrown out of her house, and even divorce. If a marriage must lead to a separation, often the correct procedures for divorce (*talaq*) are not followed by many South Asian communities. Unfortunately many women are not provided with food, clothing and maintenance during their *iddah* period in accordance with the *shariah*. In addition to this, many children are left without financial support from their fathers, and in significantly increasing numbers, this is the case when divorce between their parents has taken place.

Islam recognises the rights of each individual. It gives women and children protection, maintenance and honour in a dignified manner. A lack of education concerning the wife's rights perpetuates a cycle of turmoil, tension, oppression, and mistreatment within communities.

If correct education and guidance does not take place, these practices will continue to plague South Asian communities wherever they are in the world, and this will break up private and public life.

The abuse and misinterpretation of Islam not only hinders the community from progressing but also gives a bad reputation to Islam worldwide, as it falsely presents it to be a religion of oppression.

Everyone has a part to play in correcting the injustices and corrupt practices. Whether it is at a personal level or community level, in a *khutbah* (sermon), educational institute, or in the media, the rights of both the husband and the wife should be mentioned in the correct balance.

It is only when we have established a sincerely just system within our homes, where Islamic rights are enjoyed by all, and each person treats the other with kindness and consideration, that we will have started building societies and an Islamic nation that is successful, prosperous, just, and compassionate.

Allah Almighty says:

> Verily Allah will not change the condition
> Of a people until they
> Change it themselves.
> [Quran, Al-Ra'ad (Thunder), 13:11]

About the Author

Uzma Hussain was born in Pakistan and received her education mainly in England. In 2001 she began working for the Citizens Advice Bureau as a trainee advice worker, before becoming fully qualified in 2005. She continues to work in her legal advice role at the Bureau and at children's centres. She studied Islam in London under the direction of Dr Majdah Barhamein from Makkah. After being confronted with some cultural issues practised by South Asian Muslims which had nothing to do with Islam, she began research to identify the differences between culture and the genuine teachings of Islam. In 2004 she won a Hajj competition in *fiqh* and *tajweed* sponsored by Afnaan, an Islamic educational institute, and made her first Hajj trip to Makkah. She later travelled to Asia, Turkey and the Middle East. Throughout her travels, she continued to work on her research, drawing further understanding and insights from her experiences in different cultures.